Cambridge Elements

Elements in Shakespeare and Pedagogy
edited by
Liam E. Semler
The University of Sydney
Gillian Woods
University of Oxford

TEACHING SHAKESPEARE'S EMOTIONS

Anne Sophie Refskou
Aarhus University

Shaftesbury Road, Cambridge CB2 8EA, United Kingdom

One Liberty Plaza, 20th Floor, New York, NY 10006, USA

477 Williamstown Road, Port Melbourne, VIC 3207, Australia

314–321, 3rd Floor, Plot 3, Splendor Forum, Jasola District Centre, New Delhi – 110025, India

Cambridge University Press is part of Cambridge University Press & Assessment, a department of the University of Cambridge.

We share the University's mission to contribute to society through the pursuit of education, learning and research at the highest international levels of excellence.

www.cambridge.org
Information on this title: www.cambridge.org/9781009589505

DOI: 10.1017/9781009589512

© Anne Sophie Refskou 2026

This publication is in copyright. Subject to statutory exception and to the provisions of relevant collective licensing agreements, no reproduction of any part may take place without the written permission of Cambridge University Press & Assessment.

When citing this work, please include a reference to the DOI 10.1017/9781009589512

First published 2026

A catalogue record for this publication is available from the British Library

A Cataloging-in-Publication data record for this Element is available from the Library of Congress

ISBN 978-1-009-58950-5 Paperback
ISSN 2632-816X (online)
ISSN 2632-8151 (print)

Cambridge University Press & Assessment has no responsibility for the persistence or accuracy of URLs for external or third-party internet websites referred to in this publication and does not guarantee that any content on such websites is, or will remain, accurate or appropriate.

For EU product safety concerns, contact us at Calle de José Abascal, 56, 1°, 28003 Madrid, Spain, or email eugpsr@cambridge.org

Teaching Shakespeare's Emotions

Elements in Shakespeare and Pedagogy

DOI: 10.1017/9781009589512
First published online: March 2026

Anne Sophie Refskou
Aarhus University

Author for correspondence: Anne Sophie Refskou, litasr@cc.au.dk

ABSTRACT: Drawing on critical insights from the history of emotions and Shakespearean emotion studies, this Element offers a pedagogy rooted in a historicist approach as a stimulating alternative to the teaching of Shakespeare's emotions as universally and transhistorically relatable. It seeks to provide a roadmap – by way of contextual and analytical frameworks and suggested learning activities – for teaching students how to mind the gap between Shakespeare's emotional moment and their own. The benefits to this approach include not only students' enhanced understanding of Shakespeare's plays in the context of early modern emotion culture but also their enhanced ability to think historically and critically about emotions, both in Shakespeare's day and now.

KEYWORDS: Shakespeare, pedagogy, emotion, history, defamiliarization

© Anne Sophie Refskou 2026

ISBNs: 9781009589505 (PB), 9781009589512 (OC)
ISSNs: 2632-816X (online), 2632-8151 (print)

Contents

	Introduction	1
1	Shakespeare and the History of Emotions	14
2	Hot Emotions in *Romeo and Juliet*	23
3	Emotion, Motion and Commotion in *Julius Caesar*	43
4	Melancholy in *Twelfth Night*	59
	Conclusion	80
	References	82

Introduction

Emotions are everywhere in Shakespeare's plays. From Romeo and Juliet's love to Hamlet's grief, Othello's or Leontes' jealousy, Macbeth's guilt, Coriolanus' anger – the list of characters or situations that are defined or remembered by their distinct emotions is endless. Emotions fuel dramatic plots, motivate action, and sometimes establish the atmosphere of a play right from the beginning. In the opening scene of *Hamlet*, for instance, the two guards' jumpy fear and apprehensive emotions immediately transport the audience to the gloomy, angst-ridden place that is Shakespeare's Elsinore. In *The Merchant of Venice*, the opening line spoken by Antonio – 'In sooth I know not why I am so sad' (1.1.1) – not only tells the audience that Antonio is a 'gloomy' character but also infuses the whole play – despite it being a comedy – with an air of seemingly inexplicable sadness. Shakespearean characters react to each other 'feelingly' and they act on their feelings too, seeking revenge when they feel wronged or wooing when they are in love. They share their feelings with the audience, establishing the intimate connection between stage and auditorium that is so characteristic of Shakespearean dramaturgy through the communication of emotion in soliloquies and direct address. Think of Viola in *Twelfth Night* confessing her love for Orsino to the audience, or Hamlet repeatedly sharing his frustration and self-doubt with the auditorium.

Frequently, emotions provide a way into Shakespeare's world for students too, catching their attention and sparking their imagination. During an introductory session on Shakespeare for Danish sixth-form students (aged between sixteen and nineteen), I asked the group about their previous experience with Shakespeare – had they read any plays, seen any plays performed on the stage, and if so, what did they notice? Among the smart and sometimes surprising responses, one student expressed fascination with the emotions in *King Lear*, having recently seen a theatre production of that play. To this seventeen or eighteen-year-old, the emotional landscape created by Shakespeare and expressed by the actors on the stage was both alien and familiar, and in a word which I believe conveyed something of the student's enthusiasm, 'big'. Anyone who has ever taught Shakespeare at almost any level will no doubt have experienced similar reactions from students. Shakespeare's emotions, big and small, are often the first thing students notice in a play and the last thing they forget.

Shakespearean pedagogy from primary school level upwards has long seized upon the possibility of engaging students by paying attention to the emotional content of the plays and especially by promoting the idea of an emotional kinship with Shakespeare's characters: when students are encouraged to identify with the emotions expressed by Juliet, say, or Hamlet, the text feels relevant to them, which in turn helps them overcome the obstacles of unfamiliar historical and linguistic terrains. This approach has been championed by Rex Gibson's foundational Shakespeare in Schools Project at Cambridge University, which has been deservedly influential and has helped shift Shakespearean pedagogies in extremely fruitful ways, not least by encouraging teachers to create active classrooms inspired by theatrical practice. In the introduction to his *Teaching Shakespeare* handbook, first published in 1998 and again in a second edition in 2016, Gibson asserts that

> [i]n empathetic enactments and discussion, students gain access to the feelings of Shakespeare's characters caught up in their particular predicaments. The emotions expressed reach across the centuries: love, hate, awe, tenderness, anger, despair, jealousy, contempt, fear, courage, wonder. The settings of the plays may be remote: Caesar's Rome, medieval Scotland, an imaginary island. The dilemmas may be extreme: Juliet fearful of drinking a 'poisoned' potion, a Scottish warlord about to kill his king, an Athenian workman magically transformed into a donkey. But students make immediate connection with emotions and motivations that link with their own feelings and experience. Shakespeare's times were very different from our own, but human emotions are common to all ages. (2016, pp. 2–3)

For Gibson, teaching Shakespeare's emotions is key to helping students get past the apparent 'remoteness' of the plays. Shakespeare's emotions, it would seem by this account, are not bound or constrained by history;

rather, they transcend the gap between his historical moment and ours, and when students 'feel' with Shakespeare's characters, they are able to understand them better. This approach can unquestionably be productive in the classroom, yet, as we shall see, long-held beliefs in Shakespeare's timeless relevance – including the universal applicability of how he dramatizes human emotions – also have some distinct limits and drawbacks. Moreover, there is an alternative way to think about and teach Shakespeare's emotions, one which – I will argue in this Element – is still more productive, both critically and pedagogically.

In the course of the past three decades, Shakespeare scholars have in fact questioned the idea that 'human emotions are common to all ages' by demonstrating that the emotions we encounter in the plays and poems are instead firmly situated within the historical and cultural moment of Shakespeare's writing and are in many ways alien to twenty-first-century experience. Much of this scholarship has taken place at the intersection of Shakespeare studies and the historical discipline known as 'The History of Emotions', and it reflects a wider interdisciplinary interest in emotions and their significance in the humanities and social sciences.[1] Since the early 2000s, the historical study of emotion has become an expansive and prolific field with the establishing of several major international research centres, including the Centre for the History of the Emotions at Queen Mary University of London (established in 2008), the Centre for the History of Emotions at the Max Planck Institute (2008–2024), the Australian Research Council Centre of Excellence for the History of Emotions (2011–2018), and the Centre of Excellence in the History of Experiences at Tampere

---

[1] The wide-ranging critical interest in the emotions, which began from about the early 2000s onwards, is sometimes referred to as the 'emotional turn' or the 'affective turn' and encompasses a highly diverse set of theories and methodological approaches. A simple Google search shows how many different critical fields currently proclaim an emotional or affective turn – including history, sociology, psychology, medicine, journalism, political science, museum studies and many more. For differing analyses of the affective or emotional turn in the humanities and social sciences, see for example, Clough and Halley, 2007; Lemmings and Brooks, 2014; and Leys, 2017.

University Finland (established in 2018).[2] Explaining how emotions came to be a key topic for historians, emotion historian Rob Boddice asserts that '[t]he historian's role has come to include an appraisal of what it was like to *be* in the past: they have come to ask, what did it *feel* like' (2023, p. 10).[3] As Boddice observes, this critical and analytical shift assumes that the historian's task is not only to study the events of the past but also to study the structures of *experience* in the past. That is, what it might have felt like for people in the past to experience the world and themselves in it.

Importantly, emotion history helps us notice the ways in which emotional experience is situated by, and contingent on, a multitude of different factors. The central claim made by emotion historians is that emotions are not only hard-wired biological mechanisms but that they are also conditioned by social and cultural circumstances and discourses. This means that, far from being 'common to all ages', emotions do in fact change over time. We can learn a great deal from observing those changes. Studying emotions as a historical category, practically speaking, means, for example, asking how and why people in the past have placed value on certain emotions and sought to repress or eradicate others. The work of emotion historians can help to understand where many of the (mis)conceptions of emotions that still operate in modern societies come from, such as the idea that emotions are 'bad' because they are the opposite of reason and rationality, or the prejudice that women, for good or ill, are more 'emotional' than men. Such notions, even when we disagree with them, can have a tangible impact on how we experience our own emotions or those of others. Both men and

---

[2] The homepages of many of these centres provide a wealth of information, which has great value for teachers and students, including blogs, videos and podcasts. I have frequently directed students to 'The Emotions Lab' by the Queen Mary Centre for the History of the Emotions, which offers historical insights into individual emotions such as 'Love' or 'Anger' with short accessible essays, podcasts and visual material.

[3] See also Boddice's introduction to *The History of Emotions* (2nd ed., 2023), Katie Barclay's article 'State of the Field: The History of Emotions' (2021), or Thomas Dixon's *The History of Emotions: A Very Short Introduction* (2023) for helpful overviews of the development of the field.

women, for example, may experience certain emotions as negative and seek to suppress them for fear of being misconstrued according to gendered stereotypes. In other words, thinking about the differences between emotional experience in the past and in the present gives us perspective on our own emotions and enables us to reflect on our own circumstances rather than accepting – or insisting – that what we feel is simply what everyone else feels too.

Emotion historians also study the ways in which vocabularies of emotion change over time. Some emotion words fall out of fashion – today we tend not to use words like 'choler' or 'melancholy' very frequently, for example. Yet both these words were very familiar emotion words to Shakespeare and his contemporaries. We may assume that the emotion we call 'anger' is commonly understood throughout history. Yet, as the emotion historian Thomas Dixon puts it, the history of anger shows a 'radical discontinuity of experiences, ideas and expressions across time and cultures' (2020, p. 2), which makes it hard to assert that there is such a thing as a universal or essential kind of 'anger'. And this in turn obliges us to look more closely at how particular experiences of 'anger' – of being angry ourselves or finding that others are angry with us – are constituted and evaluated at different times.

Recognitions of this kind have also been key to emotion-centred criticism in the study of Shakespeare and his contemporaries. This said, theoretical and methodological concepts from The History of Emotions do not always map directly onto the study of Shakespeare's works, as I will explain further in the section following this introduction. This is partly because The History of Emotions is a discipline developed by historians for studying historical data rather than literary texts. Nonetheless, its key critical claims continue to chime with the ways in which many scholars now read the emotional content in Shakespeare's works. In the introduction to an important volume of essays published during the foundational phase of Shakespearean and early modern emotion studies, the editors Gail Kern Paster, Katherine Rowe and Mary Floyd-Wilson asked: 'Do the emotions in the period and place we now designate [...] as "early modern Europe" have a character and distinctive profile – an "emotional universe" – such as anthropologists describe for societies under their professional gaze?'

(2004, p. 1). Today, the answer to that question looks very much like a resounding yes. Entering the unfamiliar emotional universe inhabited by Shakespeare and his contemporaries has proved to be a thoroughly exciting journey. Shakespeare scholars have worked at – and continue to work at – gaining access to the lived experience of the historical subjects for whom Shakespeare wrote, not by assuming an easy emotional identification with the past but by recognizing that early modern people felt the world, and themselves in it, differently from the way people have done in other historical periods, including ours.

The aim of this Element is to bring some of these important critical insights into the Shakespearean classroom and to offer a pedagogy rooted in a historicist approach as a stimulating alternative to the teaching of Shakespeare's emotions as universally and transhistorically relatable. Throughout the Element, I will seek to provide a roadmap – by way of contextual and analytical frameworks and suggested learning activities – for teaching students how to mind the gap between Shakespeare's emotional moment and their own. The benefits to this approach, I will argue, include not only students' enhanced understanding of Shakespeare's plays in the context of early modern emotion culture but also their enhanced ability to think historically and critically about emotions rather than relying on easy assumptions of universality and sameness. I will show how students may gain a vocabulary for discussing emotions in the plays with precision and intellectual curiosity, while their close-reading skills are supported by frameworks that they may also apply independently when preparing for learning activities, such as in-class presentations or written assessments, such as essays and larger written projects. Through a constructive challenge to the idea of emotional familiarity, I hope to show how thinking about Shakespeare in this way will help students reflect on their own emotions, not because the ones they see on the page are the *same* as their own, but precisely because they are *different*.

Furthermore, I would argue, universalist assumptions about Shakespeare's emotions – the idea, however beguiling, that anyone, anywhere and anytime, can relate to the emotional lives of his characters – might in fact underplay present-day students' tangible ability to think both about Shakespeare *and* about emotions in nuanced and diverse ways. Would twenty-first-century students assume, or accept, the heterosexual attraction between Romeo and Juliet as universally representative of the emotion called 'Love'? In my experience, they are more likely to want to discuss the play's representation of diverse loving relationships, not all of which conform to the heterosexual model. Twenty-first-century students reading *Othello* might soon notice that the love between Othello and Desdemona is not simply self-contained and expressive of a universal idea of 'Love', but conditioned and complicated by the rules and norms of Venetian society, including its racial prejudices. Students will also be interested, I believe, in discussing why a character such as Richard III feels excluded from what he sees as certain rituals of 'Love' practised by his able-bodied co-characters. In other words, many students today are already well equipped to think about emotions not in universalist terms but rather as experiences that are both shaped by and shape diverse forms of social identity.

Ayanna Thompson and Laura Turchi have encouraged the productive acknowledgement of today's students' 'developing interest in diverse identity politics (race, gender, sexuality, physical ability)' as part of the reality of teaching Shakespeare in the twenty-first century (2016, p. 1). Several recent books on Shakespeare and Pedagogy, including Elements in this series, support this view and, like Thompson and Turchi, offer helpful critical and practical tools to support a nuanced engagement with social identities in the Shakespearean classroom.[4] In this Element, I also seek to show how and why it matters to question universalist assumptions about the Shakespearean text and its content – in this case, its emotional content – in the classroom. Like all researchers and teachers of Shakespeare, I enthusiastically believe in Shakespeare's value within the curriculum and as a superb vehicle for learning how to engage with the complexity of human existence. But I also believe that this value comes from the fact that the emotions in his texts are contingent rather than universal. As Thompson and Turchi put it,

> [o]ne can make an argument for Shakespeare's value even if that argument is not couched in universality. It is important

---

[4] See for example Panjwani, 2022; Dadabhoy and Mehdizadeh, 2023; and Whipday, 2023.

> to remember, after all, that our twenty-first-century advanced learners value the explicit exploration of identity in its many facets, and these explorations frequently and justly challenge claims of universality (after all, it is fair to ask if all teenage girls should relate to Ophelia, or if all black boys should see themselves in Hamlet). (2016, pp. 7–8)

Moreover, Ambereen Dadabhoy and Nedda Mehdizadeh point out the danger in teachers assuming Shakespeare's universal relevance, when many students find that their own experience does not fit the model laid out by the Shakespearean text and, in the case of racialization, is demonized by it.[5]

The critical impetus of historical emotion studies, I would argue, offers a valuable perspective on, and methodology for, this wider discussion of thinking inclusively about diverse identities in the Shakespearean classroom instead of relying on assumptions of universality. Importantly, emotion history does not simply encourage looking to history for 'lessons' about emotion. Rather, as Boddice stresses, by demonstrating the contingency of emotions in the past, emotion history enables nuanced thinking in and about the present:

> History challenges presentist assumptions about what people think they know. It takes common knowledge and common sense and shows them to be situated knowledge and situated sense. What counts as 'normal' or 'natural' is only ever normal or natural under certain circumstances. History disrupts such categories. (2023, p. 10)

We might also refer to this critical process as a kind of defamiliarization – a 'making strange' – which I believe has crucial value for learning processes

---

[5] Dadabhoy and Mehdizadeh, 2023, p. 12. Dadabhoy and Mehdizadeh propose the concept of 'salience' as an alternative to the relevance paradigm, which, they explain, helps to destabilize the fixity of the Shakespearean text as an expression of universal experience.

too. In their edited collection on *Teaching Social Justice through Shakespeare*, Hillary Eklund and Wendy Beth Hyman emphasize the importance of defamiliarization as a learning mode, especially the kind of defamiliarization that happens through an encounter with the historical past and its literature:

> The low-stakes testing of assumptions and taking of risks in the classroom prepare students for higher-stakes ethical and creative responses to their experience of the world. But historical literature offers us something additionally fruitful: the chance to defamiliarize our own lived experience. (2019, pp. 6–7)

Defamiliarization, Eklund and Hyman further argue, fosters 'ethical engagement with the strange or remote' (2019, p. 7), because it highlights for students the fundamental contingency of the knowledge systems we might otherwise take for granted. Teaching Shakespeare's emotions from a historicist perspective promises to do something similar. That is to say, if students recognize that Shakespeare and his contemporaries 'felt things' differently – that Shakespearean emotions may sometimes look 'strange' from a modern perspective – and if they, together with their teachers, explore this strangeness with open-minded intellectual curiosity, the resulting conversation promises to stimulate their awareness and tolerance of the diverse emotions they themselves feel and encounter, both in the classroom and beyond.

In this Element, I view the twenty-first-century Shakespearean classroom as a diverse 'affective space', one into which students bring their differing experiences and understandings of emotional identity. I understand 'space' not only as the physical environment designed (or not designed) for teaching but also as a dynamic concept. As the emotion historian Katie Barclay observes, 'space' is a process; it is something that happens at the intersection of 'physical environment, human behaviour and discourse' (2017, p. 21). Thus, the understanding of space is closely related to the understanding of emotion because people bring their emotions into a physical environment – or react and behave emotionally within that environment – which contributes to the process of turning that environment into a 'space'. In the classroom, the emotions of teachers and students and the different cultural and social discourses that inform their emotions are what turn the classroom into a highly complex 'affective space'. This process can be wonderfully productive for the exchange of knowledge and opinion that is foundational to learning, and it can create tension too when different behaviours and discourses collide. Introducing the historicized study of Shakespeare's emotions into the affective space of the classroom can help both students and teachers to negotiate and inhabit this space, I believe, because this learning mode detaches Shakespeare's emotions from normative categories and assumptions and, in doing so, supports awareness and tolerance of emotional diversity in a broader sense.

The Element is organized as follows: this introduction is followed by a section that provides a short overview of the intersection of historical emotion studies and Shakespeare studies, and which begins to suggest how we might put into practice the process of historicizing early modern emotions in the classroom. This is then followed by three 'practice' sections, each focusing on a frequently taught Shakespearean play: *Romeo and Juliet*, *Julius Caesar* and *Twelfth Night*. The selected plays work as case studies for exploring a key early modern emotion discourse as a contextual framework for teaching Shakespeare. In the section on *Romeo and Juliet*, I introduce humoral theory with its insistence on some emotional temperaments as 'hot' or 'cold', 'wet' or 'dry', and suggest ways in which students might analyse the 'emotional temperatures' at work in the play – exploring for example why emotions such as love and anger are described as 'hot', and why this in turn matters for understanding the play's dramatization of emotion and gender. In the section on *Julius Caesar*, I discuss the early modern understanding of emotions as tangible forces that would set bodies in motion both on the inside and on the outside. Highlighting the etymological connections between 'emotion', 'motion', and 'commotion', I show how students may gain a historically situated understanding of how emotions work – how they *move* people – in the play. I also extend this contextual and analytical framework to learning activities designed to enhance students' understanding of the early modern theatre as a space full of '(e)motion'. Finally, in the section on *Twelfth Night*, I look at melancholy as one of the most important – and, to modern eyes, 'strange' – emotion-related conditions in the early modern period. Melancholy is a key component in Shakespeare's emotional vocabulary too, and understanding what 'melancholy' meant to Shakespeare's contemporaries helps students to pursue a historically informed engagement with his writing. Studying the fascinating early modern discourse of melancholy offers students a productively defamiliarizing perspective on the complexity of feeling 'sad', both in Shakespeare's day and now. In this section, I also address the relationship between emotion, melancholy, and gender in *Twelfth Night*, offering perspectives and suggesting learning activities that may help teachers and students to pursue this issue when studying the play.

In each of the three 'practice' sections, I suggest additional plays from the Shakespearean canon which may be taught by drawing on the contextual framework outlined in the section, in the assumption that teachers will wish to adapt and suit some of the ideas to a wider range of plays. The focus of this Element is primarily on the teaching of Shakespeare's plays, but its historicist pedagogy could productively be applied to the teaching of the *Sonnets* and Shakespeare's other poems too. The *Sonnets* certainly offer rich material for emotion-oriented analysis, and I hope that teachers will see the potential for adapting the contents of this Element for their own purposes. In addition to suggested learning activities, each section includes a list of relevant student-friendly background texts that may be included in course materials, such as course packs. What teachers at all levels typically lack more than anything is time. Sourcing and selecting reading lists for new courses and modules is inspiring and pleasurable, but it is also time-consuming, and so I have tried to do some of this work for colleagues.

I draw on my own research experience throughout this Element: much of my scholarly work to date has been informed by, and has sought to develop, historical emotion studies as a subfield within Shakespeare studies. I also draw on my own teaching experience, which includes teaching on undergraduate and postgraduate programmes – in English and Comparative Literature and in Theatre and Performance studies – primarily in the UK and Denmark, as well as an ongoing engagement with Danish general upper secondary education, the Danish *gymnasium*, where students aged 16–19 who have selected to study English at the equivalent of the UK's A-level will typically study Shakespeare in their third and final year. Drawing on my own background, then, I have organized this Element primarily with English and Comparative Literature and, to a lesser degree, Theatre and Performance Studies in mind. Most of the suggested learning activities support student skills in close reading and literary analysis and encourage them to work with early modern source texts. All the learning activities are intended to take place during teaching sessions, but some may be adapted to give to students as written assignments or as set tasks to guide their reading in preparation for class. Generally speaking, the learning activities are designed to provide inspiration through a flexible format – the 'instructions' I give are by no means set in stone and, I hope, may be adapted to suit different teaching contexts and levels.

The Element is designed to be applicable to Shakespeare and early modern drama courses primarily at university level, although I hope it may also appeal to teachers in higher secondary education, such as British sixth-form colleges and their international equivalents. I realize that time restrictions and other pressures at all educational institutions do not allow teachers to focus solely or extensively on emotions in Shakespeare, yet, as I began by noting, emotions are likely to feature somehow in students' responses to – and discussions of – the text, and I hope the Element may be of use by providing frameworks for such responses and discussions. I also believe that the prompt to think historically about emotions in Shakespeare's works may be of value for the several different contexts in which Shakespeare is 'taught', such as the theatre rehearsal room, the museum, or other cultural heritage organizations. The contents of this Element may also be useful for teaching in 'new' interdisciplinary fields such as the medical and health humanities, where literature and the arts meet medical science and practice, and where Shakespeare has been deployed as a literary vehicle for teaching emotional empathy in doctor-patient scenarios.[6] One issue with using Shakespeare and other literary texts in this particular context is a potentially reductive instrumentalization of the text, one that overlooks or occludes its historicity, especially if Shakespeare is directly 'applied' to modern-day emotional contexts and used as a resource of transhistorical wisdom. The critical approach of this

---

[6] See for example Jeffrey, 2021; Pang, Thrichelvam, and Wider, 2023.

Element, I hope, offers a constructive way to avoid this issue by demonstrating the pedagogical value of systematically addressing and exploring the historicity of Shakespeare's emotions.

Teaching early modern emotions offers the possibility of teaching across the aesthetic disciplines – literature, drama, painting, music – but it also requires engaging with the inherently 'interdisciplinary' nature of early modern thinking in general. The divisions between the arts and the 'hard' sciences, so familiar to us today, do not apply when we work within an early modern context, because the disciplinary separations that inform our modern educational and professional systems were not yet in place in the sixteenth and seventeenth centuries. In the case of melancholy, for example, students will find that what they might understand primarily as 'literature' and what they might understand as 'medicine' cannot be easily untangled in the early modern texts that sought to understand and define this emotional phenomenon. This experience may produce a certain confusion at first reading, but it also offers the possibility of engaging students in a historically-informed reflection on what it means to think and work across different disciplines. Modern interdisciplinary fields such as the medical humanities are pushing for a valuable and productive encounter between the arts and medicine; teachers and students who are interested in pursuing this critical and pedagogical direction will find that in early modern texts, some of the roadmap is already laid out, simply because the disciplinary ground is already a shared one.

Finally, and importantly, this Element is intended to support students at various levels and across different educational contexts in becoming active practitioners of emotion history rather than recipients within a passive learning situation. A fundamental principle in my own pedagogical practice has always been to provide students with ready-to-use 'tools' – both critical and methodological – so that they are well equipped to think and work independently and pursue the topics that interest them the most (rather than just the topics that interest me). This Element is based on that principle too. It is my hope that its contents will help teachers encourage their students to continue to explore new topics and sources relevant to understanding emotions in Shakespeare's plays in a historical context. Much work has been done at the intersection of historical emotion studies and Shakespeare studies, but there is still a great deal more to do. I believe that if we, as teachers, can share with students the exciting and intellectually stimulating task of uncovering the emotional past in Shakespeare's plays, the ground will be laid for future projects in the field.

1 Shakespeare and the History of Emotions

The purpose of this section is to expand on key critical and methodological aspects of the historical study of Shakespeare's emotions, and to introduce some of the most frequently cited early modern source texts on emotion. Towards the end of the section, I include a learning activity intended to introduce students to working with an early modern source text on emotion and thus to demonstrate where we might begin with the historical study of emotions in the Shakespearean classroom, practically speaking. The activity asks students to read an extract from Thomas Wright's seventeenth-century treatise *The Passions of the Mind in General* and to compare its descriptions of the emotional workings of the human heart with contemporary understandings and representations of emotions and the 'heart', including their own. The comparison is intended to facilitate students' discovery of the vast and fascinating divide between the 'then' and 'now' of emotional experience, hopefully stimulating their intellectual curiosity as part of the process. The section thus provides material that I hope may inspire and facilitate an introductory teaching session – such as a lecture or a seminar – on the historical study of Shakespeare's emotions. I also include a list of useful background reading at the end of the section, which may be used in course pack material, and which is intended to save teachers time in sourcing and selecting texts.

As I noted in the introduction, Shakespeare scholars interested in the historical study of emotions have relatively rarely applied the methodological concepts developed by emotion historians directly to the study of drama and poetry by Shakespeare and his contemporaries.[7] There is

---

[7] Notable exceptions in this context includes Erin Sullivan, whose scholarship demonstrates the value of explicit terminological crossovers from the History of Emotions to the study of Shakespearean and early modern literature (see Sullivan,

a fundamental disciplinary divide between the ways in which emotion historians study large (or small) collections of sources and the ways in which Shakespeare scholars study a literary text, such as a play or a poem. Shakespeare scholars study a wide range of non-literary sources too, but they usually study such sources contextually with a view to analysing their primary literary text. Shakespearean emotion studies have thus largely developed their own set of analytical foci and methodologies, which are not necessarily shared with the wider field of emotion history, even if there is a common critical impetus in the wish to historicize emotions. The critical interest in Shakespearean and early modern emotions took flight in the 1990s and has since continued to develop and expand into a now firmly established sub-field of Shakespeare studies, as Katharine Craik's important collection of essays on *Shakespeare and Emotion* (2020) attests. The early stage of the field was strongly influenced by the foundational work of scholars such as Gail Kern Paster (1993, 1998, 2004), Michael Schoenfeldt (1999), and Paster, Rowe, and Floyd-Wilson (2004). Paster's work, in particular, paved the way for a new critical engagement with humoral theory as a key paradigm for reading Shakespearean and early modern emotions, an approach which continues to inform the contextual and analytical toolkit of the Shakespearean emotion scholar, as Section 2 of this Element will show. Following Paster, other scholars have argued for a broader contextual framework, looking beyond humoral theory and the emphasis on early modern emotion as an embodied experience, which came with the focus on humoral theory.[8]

More recently, important developments in Shakespearean emotion studies have included the focus on 'positive' emotions – such as joy, pleasure, and happiness – rather than the negative emotions – such as fear, grief, and

---

2016), and Marion A. Wells, who usefully integrates the work of, among others, Rosenwein into her comparative study of classical, medieval and early modern literature (see Wells, 2023).

[8] See Cummings and Sierhuis (2013), and Meek and Sullivan (2015). I explain humoral theory and the focus on early emotions as embodied in further detail in Section 2.

melancholy – which tended to dominate earlier phases.[9] Recently, scholars have also established productive critical intersections with other topics of current interest to Shakespeare studies. Carol Mejia LaPerle has shown ways in which to redress Shakespearean emotions from the perspective of Premodern Critical Race Studies (2019, 2022); Kristine Steenbergh has pointed towards the presence of more-than-human emotions in Shakespeare's poetry (2022); and Bradley Irish has shown the methodological value of marrying knowledge from the modern affective sciences with the historicist approach typically deployed by Shakespearean emotion scholars (2023). As these new directions demonstrate, the study of Shakespeare's emotions continues to develop, typically with a firm grounding in the historicist premise that also informs the pedagogy argued by this Element and, at the same time, finding new ways to look at Shakespeare's emotions from an increasingly interdisciplinary perspective.

Emotions or Passions?

Early modern people, speaking about their emotions, sometimes deployed different terms and meanings from the vocabularies we use today. As emotion historians often point out, in the seventeenth century, the word 'emotion' was only just beginning to mean what we generally take it to mean today. The *Oxford English Dictionary* currently defines 'emotion' as 'strong mental or instinctive feeling, as pleasure, grief, hope, fear etc.' (*OED* 3a), which I assume sounds familiar to most twenty-first-century readers. However, Shakespeare never uses the word 'emotion'. Instead, he uses words such as 'passions' or 'affections'. These words do cover meanings closely related to modern understandings of emotion – 'anger' or 'love', for example, are named as 'passions' in Shakespeare's plays – but passions and emotions can also be rather different phenomena. As I will show throughout the different sections of this Element, early modern culture had some quite specific and systematic understandings of what passions were and how they worked. This does not mean that it is necessarily wrong to use the word 'emotion' when analysing and discussing

---

[9] On positive emotions in early modern literature and culture, see Fox, Irish, and Miura (2021).

early modern texts, including those written by Shakespeare; many scholars use emotion as a general term, not least for the sake of clarity, and I will do the same throughout this Element.[10] However, the mere fact that Shakespeare uses different words where we use the word emotion alerts us to a gap between his emotional moment and ours, and it is usually one of the first points I highlight in a teaching context in order to encourage students to think about that gap as one partly defined by language.

Furthermore, for historians of early modern emotion, especially those influenced by the foundational work of Gail Kern Paster, emotions do not just change conceptually or discursively, but also phenomenologically, because discourse is integral to phenomenological experience. Drawing on the phenomenological philosophy of Maurice Merleau-Ponty, Paster has argued that 'the nature of an individual subject's phenomenological experience can never be understood properly apart from the social field in which it takes place and thus apart from that social field's governing beliefs about how the world is constituted' (2004, p. 8). What this means, put more simply, is that the ways in which people speak about emotions – how they name them and describe them – inevitably influence how they experience them. Simultaneously, people's descriptions of emotion are influenced by what Paster calls the 'social field' – that is, the beliefs, understandings, and norms that are specific to different cultures and historical periods. In other words, we might feel emotion as a physiological reaction – a tension in the stomach or the shoulders from fear, a sudden facial warmth from shame or embarrassment – but the embodied experience of emotion is deeply entangled with the stories we have been told about fear, shame, and embarrassment.

Sources of Early Modern Emotion

Scholars have uncovered multiple intellectual traditions in the early modern landscape of emotion and continue to do so. This is not least to do with the fact that the early modern period was particularly interested in emotion and

---

[10] For a helpful and pragmatic discussion of 'emotions' as a general term, while at the same time acknowledging the historical use of other terms such as passions and affections, see Rosenwein, 2006, pp. 3–5.

therefore produced a great deal of printed texts which today constitute important sources for scholars. A whole new genre of writings on emotion – in which writers discussed both distinct emotions and theorized about the nature of emotion in general – began in this period. As Benedict Robinson remarks, the first books exclusively devoted to the passions since antiquity were in fact produced in the seventeenth century (2021, p. 27). The authors of these books and treatises, some of whom I will cite throughout this Element, drew on a very wide range of ideas from classical literature, medicine, philosophy, theology, and other traditions in ways that to the modern reader may appear unsystematic, even chaotic. Nor do they always present their views on emotion in a consistent manner; an opinion put forward on one page may be contradicted a few pages later. Moreover, the early modern vocabulary and spelling can be a challenge for students, but as sources providing access to the early modern experience of emotion, these texts are invaluable, and, in my experience, students will often find the opportunity to explore primary sources a rewarding one. The list of English texts most frequently referred to by Shakespearean scholars interested in emotion include Thomas Wright's *The Passions of the Mind in General* (first published in 1601 and in an enlarged edition in 1604 with reissued editions in 1621 and 1630); Nicholas Coeffeteau, *A Table of Human Passions with their Causes and Effects* (translated from French into English, 1621); Edward Reynolds, *A Treatise of the Passions and Faculties of the Soul of Man* (1640), and two texts exclusively dedicated to the study of melancholy: Timothy Bright's *A Treatise on Melancholy* (1586), and Robert Burton's *The Anatomy of Melancholy* (first published in 1621 and in multiple subsequent editions).

These texts are all available online, with digitized images of early printed editions and (mostly) in transcription, on the subscription ProQuest database Early English Books Online (EEBO). Alternatively, the 'Early English Books Online Collections' by the University of Michigan Library provides free access to transcriptions, and, like EEBO, allows the user to search for specific words and phrases in the texts, as does the (also free) database 'EarlyPrint: Curating and Exploring Early Printed English' created by Northwestern University and Washington University in St. Louis. Moreover, the free online resource 'Sources of Early Modern Emotion in English 1500–1700' generously provides bibliographies of primary sources related to single emotions – such as love, melancholy, anger, and so on – as well as extensive bibliographies of recent scholarship on early modern emotion. There is thus a great deal of online material and resources available for teachers and students studying Shakespearean and early modern emotions, and I will suggest different ways in which students may access and use this material throughout this Element.

When reading primary sources on early modern emotion alongside Shakespeare's plays, it is important for students to understand that the plays do not necessarily express or represent these sources in any straightforward or orthodox manner. In fact, part of what makes Shakespeare's emotions so exciting to trace and discuss is the way in which he dramatizes (and sometimes contradicts and challenges) emotion discourses present in early modern culture. Shakespeare always seems to cherry-pick elements from different contemporary beliefs about emotions in a less than systematic manner, constructing an eclectic set of emotional idioms for his characters. At the same time, we may also read the plays as emotional investigations in the sense that their author is *searching* for an understanding of emotions, questioning what emotions do, rather than presenting or promoting any individual emotion theory. In other words, I believe that it is both important and rewarding to encourage students to identify instances of early modern emotion discourses in the plays, but it is equally important to ask students to think about how the plays shape and reshape these discourses.

The Heart of Early Modern Emotion: A Learning Activity

As I will show in the 'practice' section focused on *Romeo and Juliet*, early modern passions were widely believed to reside in the different organs of the human body – an explicitly embodied understanding of emotion which is somewhat different from how we tend to imagine the emotions now, even if we acknowledge the physical effect they may have on us. One of the organs that was believed to 'house' the passions was the human heart. This may not come as a great surprise to students; after all, if there is one organ that we still associate with emotional experience, it is indeed the heart. A Google search for images related to the word 'love' immediately produces scores of heart shapes. However, the rather specific early modern understanding of how the heart responds to the experience of different emotions *is* typically unfamiliar territory for students when they first encounter it. This activity asks students, first, to think about any connections between emotions and the human heart, 'brainstorming' in small groups and 'Googling' images or verbal examples. Questions to get students started could include:

(1) Where and how do you typically associate love with the heart?
(2) When you use the heart/broken heart emojis in text messages, what kind of work do they do, and why do you use them?
(3) When you hear or use expressions such as 'heartfelt' or 'cold/warm-hearted', what do they mean to you?

The groups may either note down their answers and findings – collecting a folder of visual and textual examples – or work together in real time by adding their ideas and examples to a shared digital board, such as 'Padlet'. When students have gathered a substantive number of examples, they should then be asked to read the following short extract from Thomas Wright's seventeenth-century treatise *The Passions of the Mind in General*:

> The very seat of all Passions, is the heart, both of men and beasts: divers reasons move me to this opinion. First the very common experience men try daily and hourly in themselves, for who loveth extremely, and feeleth not that passion to dissolve his heart? Who rejoyceth and proveth not his heart dilated? Who is moiled with heaviness, or plunged with pain, and perceiveth not his heart to be contracted? Whom inflameth ire, and hath not heart burning? By these experiences, we prove in our hearts the working of Passions, and by the noise of their tumult, we understand the work of their presence. (1604, sig. D1^r)[11]

---

[11] For the sake of readability, I have slightly modernized the spelling of this and other early modern texts and their titles throughout the Element. When asking students to find and read early modern sources on their own, I would preface the

Switching from group readings to a teacher-led discussion, I would then ask students, first of all, what they make of Wright's detailed description – what does it say about the heart and its relationship with what we would call emotions? Depending on their answers, I would then prompt them to describe why (or why not) Wright's understanding of this relationship might be different from theirs. The important takeaways from this discussion should help students to understand and formulate how the passage reminds us that:

(1) William Harvey's discovery of the heart as a blood-pumping muscle had not yet taken place when Shakespeare wrote his plays and poems[12]
(2) The connection between emotion and the heart, which we still cultivate today, had a distinctly material aspect to it in Shakespeare's day

Wright describes a heart that dissolves with love, dilates with joy, contracts with grief or pain, and burns with 'ire' or anger, and this should not to be read metaphorically – Wright's actively changing heart is not the same as the heart shapes we encounter on Google when searching for images of 'love'. Instead, this understanding of how the heart behaves when it is affected by the different passions is situated in a particular historical moment and tied to a particular understanding of emotion, which I will continue to explain and discuss throughout this Element.

Wright bases his argumentation on what he perceives as his own felt experience: 'the very common experience men try daily and hourly in themselves': the proof of his argument lies literally in his own passionate heart. A historian of early modern emotions will seriously engage with – and give due importance to – the experience that Wright here describes. To be sure, modern science will be able to contradict the validity of what Wright claims to feel and probably allocate his account to an earlier and now superseded stage of the continuous development of human knowledge

---

task with a conversation about early modern spelling to prepare students for the challenge and encourage them to adopt a persistent reading practice.

[12] William Harvey's work on the heart and the circulation of blood was published in the seminal anatomical study *De Motu Cordis* in 1628, twelve years after Shakespeare's death.

about emotion. Yet to dismiss his account as invalid because it lacks the empirical proof established by later generations would mean to dismiss the rich and complex cultural history of the ways in which humans have conceptualized their emotions and continue to do so. In the context of teaching Shakespeare's emotion, this account of what emotions *feel* like to an early modern subject is equally valuable because it provides students with a context for analysing moments in Shakespeare's plays when characters describe an emotional experience, which, like Wright's might be directly and tangibly connected to their hearts. When, for example, Othello tells Desdemona that he 'cannot speak enough of this content. / It stops me here; it is too much of joy' (2.1.214–15), is he pointing to his heart – the 'here' in the line – and would Shakespeare's audiences have assumed that he means that his heart, like Wright's, is dilated with the joy that he feels upon seeing his wife? Does he mean that his joy is heartfelt, literally speaking, and that his inability to speak further is a bodily sensation too? Is there perhaps also a slight element of danger to this expansion of Othello's heart, an emotional experience that he does not entirely control? The answers to these questions are likely to be affirmative, but the analytical process of asking them is underwritten by a historically-informed understanding of emotion and by a contextual knowledge derived from primary sources such as Wright's treatise. It is this process that I hope this Element will make accessible and applicable to the teaching of Shakespeare's emotions.

Background Reading

This list is necessarily short and far from comprehensive, given the extremely prolific nature of early modern and Shakespearean emotion studies. However, the titles listed all include highly useful and relatively student-friendly overviews and introductions either to the History of Emotions in general and/or to Shakespearean and early modern emotions. I have not included studies focused on single emotions here, since I cite and list some of these in the subsequent sections of this Element. The reading list I provide could be included in teaching materials such as course packs or given to students ahead of an introductory lecture on Shakespeare and the History of Emotions, assuming the teaching schedule allows for such a lecture.

Barclay, Katie. (2021). 'State of the Field: The History of Emotions'. *History* 106(71), 456-466

Barclay, Katie. (2020). *The History of Emotions: A Student Guide to Methods and Sources*, London: Bloomsbury.

Boddice, Rob. (2023). *The History of Emotions*, 2nd ed., Manchester: Manchester University Press.

Broomhall, Susan, ed. (2017). *Early Modern Emotions: An Introduction*, London: Routledge.

Craik, Katharine A., ed. (2020). *Shakespeare and Emotion*, Cambridge: Cambridge University Press.

Dixon, Thomas. (2023). *The History of Emotions: A Very Short Introduction*, Oxford: Oxford University Press.

Escolme, Bridget. (2014). *Emotional Excess on the Shakespearean Stage*, London: Arden Shakespeare.

Hobgood, Allison P. (2014). *Passionate Playgoing in Early Modern England*, Cambridge: Cambridge University Press.

Meek, Richard, and Sullivan, Erin, eds. (2015). *The Renaissance of Emotion: Understanding Affect in Shakespeare and his Contemporaries*, Manchester: Manchester University Press.

Paster, Gail Kern ; Rowe, Katherine, and Floyd-Wilson, Mary, eds. (2004). *Reading the Early Modern Passions: Essays in the Cultural History of Emotion*, Philadelphia: University of Pennsylvania Press.

White, R.S. ; Houlahan, Mark, and O'Loughlin, Katrina, eds. (2015). *Shakespeare and Emotions: Inheritances, Enactments, Legacies*, New York: Palgrave Macmillan.

2 Hot Emotions in *Romeo and Juliet*

The purpose of this section is to introduce early modern humoral theory as a contextual and analytical framework for facilitating students' reading of the emotion-inflected language of 'heat' in *Romeo and Juliet*.[13] 'Everyone' knows that *Romeo and Juliet* is a play about love; it is one of the most famous literary texts ever written about that emotion. But love is far from the only emotion at work in the play. The action is ostensibly driven (at least) as much by anger and hatred as by love. In fact, although the prologue tells us that the two young protagonists 'bury their parents' strife' (Prologue, 8) with their deaths – so that it looks as if love ultimately conquers hate – love and hate are not so much antithetical in the play as they are deeply intertwined. When we first meet Romeo, his words wilfully confuse the two emotions: 'Here's much to do with hate, but more with love: / Why then, O brawling love, O loving hate, / O anything of nothing first create!' (1.1.166–67), and when Juliet discovers Romeo's identity at the Capulet party, she exclaims: 'My only love sprung from my only hate!' (1.5.137). So, in *Romeo and Juliet*, love and hate are not only interchangeable, but they also appear to spring from the same source. Moreover, these two emotions work as some of the most active forces in the play, propelling the characters and the plot forward with irrepressible energy, and both emotions cause repeated and escalating acts of violence, some of which are fatal.

The explanation for the symbiotic relationship between love and hate in *Romeo and Juliet*, I will argue in this section, lies in the fact that both are considered 'hot' emotions within the framework of 'humoral theory', which was one of the governing paradigms for thinking about emotions in the early modern period. The importance of humoral theory to the early modern emotional landscape is now largely taken as a matter of fact by Shakespeare scholars, thanks to the extensive and influential scholarship of Gail Kern Paster and others, as I noted in Section 1. If we want to understand – and to teach – what emotions meant to Shakespeare and his audiences, we cannot ignore the discourse of the four humours. As Matthew Steggle puts it, '[a]t the most basic level, knowledge of the humours helps, simply, in understanding the dialogue of Shakespeare's plays' (2018, p. 224). Humoral theory is not just helpful in decoding Shakespeare's emotional idiom, however, it is, as Paster and Steggle, and other scholars observe, key

---

[13] Deep thanks to Dr Varsha Panjwani and her students at Fordham University, London for helpful comments on some of the material that went into this section.

to understanding early modern emotional selfhood.[14] The emotional experience of Shakespearean characters – the ways in which they react to the world and the ways in which they *feel* themselves in the world – is often explicitly or implicitly underwritten by humoral theory. To be sure, humoral theory is not the only paradigm or knowledge framework for understanding early modern emotions. As I noted in Section 1, some recent scholarship has questioned the strong emphasis on early modern emotions as material and embodied that is at the centre of humoral-focused readings of Shakespeare. Other discourses – from, for example, philosophy or religion – also influenced the ways in which early moderns understood their emotions. Yet it is nonetheless quite clear that when Shakespeare describes the emotional experience of his characters, he often relies on, or echoes, humorally inflected language, and it is safe to assume that his audiences would have understood that language very well indeed. They might also have thought of themselves as humoral 'beings' – that is, as feeling alternately 'hot' or 'cold', 'dry' or 'wet' depending on the constitution of their bodies and their emotions. Moreover, as I will discuss later in this section, we cannot necessarily assume a neat separation between humoral theory and other discourses in the period; rather, the humours find their way into multiple areas of early modern thinking, especially when emotions are at work.

I begin this section with a brief introduction to humoral theory and discuss what it meant for the early modern experience of emotion, before turning to *Romeo and Juliet* in order to suggest ways in which to teach the two key emotions in the play – love and hate – by deploying humoral theory as a contextual and analytical framework. Bringing humoral theory into the Shakespearean classroom is key to fulfilling the main objective of this Element, which is to significantly enhance students' understanding of Shakespeare's plays and their emotion-related content by way of a historicist pedagogy, one that situates Shakespeare's emotions within their proper historical and cultural moment rather than treating emotion as a universal human experience that transcends historical and cultural

---

[14] See Paster, 2004; and Steggle, 2018. Escolme, 2014 also draws on the humours as a key interpretative framework.

differences. Thus, as I hope this section will demonstrate, as students begin to understand why some emotions feel 'hot' or 'cold' and 'wet' or 'dry' to Shakespearean characters, they learn to discuss Shakespeare's emotions with historical specificity and to identify and describe key differences between early modern and present-day emotions.

Introducing students to humoral theory also helps achieve my other primary objective in this Element, which is to explore and deploy 'defamiliarization' as a productive mode of learning. As I argued in the introduction, the process of defamiliarization – the 'making strange' that takes place when students encounter the unfamiliar territory of early modern emotion with its distinct historicity – has pedagogical value on (at least) two levels. Students learn to appreciate the gap between the experience of emotion in Shakespeare's time and later historical periods (including now); it is also my hope that they also gain perspective on the diversity of emotional experience in general. In other words, the defamiliarizing encounter with Shakespeare's emotions in the classroom may help to produce the kind of reflexive skillset sought by Hillary Eklund and Wendy Beth Hyman for the establishment of an 'ethical engagement' with the world (2019, p. 7), as also cited in my introduction.

In humoral theory, students will almost certainly encounter a profoundly – and, I hope, intriguingly – unfamiliar understanding of emotions. Traces of the humours and their corresponding 'temperatures' are preserved in some of the expressions and vocabulary we use about emotion today – we might still imagine anger as 'hot', for instance – but the early modern understanding of the humoral body with its four basic fluid substances – blood, phlegm, choler and black bile – is distinctly 'strange' and ostensibly belongs to a different moment in medical and cultural history. At the same time, in my experience, the humoral version of what we today would call 'psychology' fascinates students, both because it is so different from a modern world view and because the highly systematic framework of the humours – which I will explain shortly – is in fact quite accessible and intellectually attractive. In the humoral understanding of the body – and of the body in the world – everything is connected, and everything, or almost everything, can be explained in terms of cause and effect. Shakespeare, not surprisingly, is by no means an orthodox proponent of humoral theory and often complicates the discourse of humoralism rather than simply reiterating it; as teachers, we should be careful not to let students assume that humoralism is an entirely straightforward key with which we may unlock the emotional content of his plays. Rather, students should be helped to understand the ways in which the humours constitute a shared system of knowledge that Shakespeare and his contemporaries drew on in order to describe and discuss emotions, *and* they should be encouraged to identify moments in the plays at which Shakespeare challenges that knowledge system.

The three learning activities suggested at the end of this section are designed to (1) facilitate students' active engagement with, and understanding of, humoral theory, and (2) guide their reading of how the humours might be at work in *Romeo and Juliet*. The key learning objective is to train students in thinking historically – and in deploying historicist method – when analysing Shakespeare's dramatization of emotion. The activities involve close reading and analysis of select examples from *Romeo and Juliet* and suggest ways in which students might explore online resources to gain information from primary texts about early modern emotion. I have suggested a flexible format and set of instructions for the activities – as well as examples of questions that will prompt students to closely read the humoral language of the play – so that they may be adapted to different teaching situations and levels. I end the section with a short list of background reading and online resources, which will provide both teachers and students with excellent information on humoral theory and Shakespeare, as well as inspiring critical discussion.

Early Modern Humoral Theory

Shakespeare and his contemporaries inherited humoral theory from classical antiquity, more specifically from the medical systems outlined by two Greek philosophers and physicians, Hippocrates (*c.* 460 – *c.* 370 BCE) and, later, Galen (129 – *c.* 216 CE): early modern humours are also often referred to as 'Galenic humours'. Humoral theory derives from the belief that all bodies contain four fluids, or 'humours': blood, phlegm, yellow bile (or choler), and black bile (or melancholy). As Danijela Kambaskovic notes, the etymological relationship between the humours and their liquid quality still resonates in the English word 'humid' (2017, p. 39). The first two key points to note about the humours, then, are that they were believed to be resident in the body as material substances and that they were thought to have a powerful impact on the body's general state of health. In humoralism, moreover, the mind and the body are closely connected, so when the humours were out of order, the mind would suffer too, as is especially evident in descriptions of early modern melancholy, as we will see in Section 4. The four humours had different qualities and were related to the four elements of air, water, fire, and earth and to the four seasons, thus connecting the human body to the wider macrocosm of the natural world. The humour of blood (air, spring) was believed to be warm and moist; the humour of phlegm (water, winter) was also moist but believed to be cold; the humour of yellow bile (fire, summer) was warm and dry; while black bile (earth, autumn) was cold and dry. From the four humours were derived the four temperaments: sanguine (blood), phlegmatic (phlegm), choleric (yellow bile), and melancholic (black bile). At the heart of much early modern medical practice – both diagnoses and cures – is the belief that all four humours should be evenly balanced in the body. If the body were to produce an excess of one of the humours, the effect would manifest as a variety of symptoms, both physical and mental.

The humours were common to all and therefore defined as 'natural' constituents of the body, but they could be influenced by the so-called 'non-naturals', which included the passions or emotions. As Katherine Rowe notes, 'like air, diet, exercise, elimination, and sleep' the passions could 'destabilize but also regulate the body's dynamic balance of cold and hot, wet and dry humors' (2003, p. 50). The experience of a particular emotion, in other words, happened in a symbiotic relationship with the humours and affected their presence in the body. The experience of anger, for example, would produce hot and dry yellow bile, or choler, and so the body would feel heated. The experience of grief or sadness, on the other hand, would produce black bile, or melancholy, and result in the body feeling increasingly cold and dry. The humours resided in and were produced by the body's internal organs. Early modern models of humoral theory do contain variants and idiosyncrasies (as students will inevitably experience when studying non-literary source texts on the topic or looking at modern diagrams online); however, blood was usually understood to be produced by the heart, phlegm by the brain, yellow bile by the liver, and black bile by the spleen. From the organs, the humours were dispersed throughout the body via the bloodstream and thus affected its different parts. As we saw in Section 1, in the extract from Thomas Wright's treatise *The Passions of the Mind in General*, emotional experience was thought to have a direct impact on the heart, and the explanation lies in the operation of the humours. An overproduction of yellow bile, for example, would send this hot and dry humour from the liver to the heart, causing a burning feeling in the latter, as we also see in Wright's description: 'Who inflameth ire, and hath not heart burning?' Or, as Paster explains, '[f]or the early moderns, emotions flood the body not metaphorically, but literally, as the humors course through the bloodstream carrying choler, melancholy, blood, and phlegm to the parts' (2004, p. 14). As is clear from Paster's phrasing, the early modern experience of emotion is more explicitly embodied than we would expect from our knowledge of modern psychology (a term which did not yet exist).

The guiding principle of modern Western thinking about the mind and the body is dualistic: by and large, we tend to imagine mind and body as separate and distinct, although some contemporary medical practice resists this division. Yet many scholars now argue that for Shakespeare and his contemporaries, there was not yet such a clear separation between the body and what we now think of as the more immaterial workings of the mind or the psyche – and hence the emotions. As Steggle explains, dualism is usually traced to the philosophical works of René Descartes in the mid seventeenth century, and although Shakespeare's pre-Cartesian world was not without dualistic ideas, it had a 'less philosophically rigorous sense of a chasm between consciousness and the material body' (2018, p. 225). For those of us who teach and study Shakespeare's works, then, this means that we need to re-situate the emotional experiences described in the texts within their proper historical and intellectual framework. Thus when the angry Westmoreland in the first scene of *Henry VI Part 3* claims that his 'heart for anger burns' (1.1.60) or Captain Fluellen in *Henry V* is 'touched with choler, hot as gunpowder' (4.7.170), we might choose to read their statements as metaphorical – again, the idea of anger as hot and explosive has survived in our vocabulary, so the connection should be quite familiar to us – but we might also choose to read such expressions as coming from an embodied experience of feeling angry. Anger, or choler, *feels* hot to Westmoreland and Fluellen because their bodies are producing a great deal of yellow bile, and so their language intermixes metaphor and materiality – word and feeling – in ways that are *not* so familiar to us.

Most authors of books and treatises on the passions in the sixteenth and seventeenth centuries incorporate humoral theory into their theorizing about the passions and acknowledge the close relationship between the two. Elsewhere in *The Passions of the Mind in General*, Wright refers directly to the humours in order to advocate regulation and moderation of the passions:

> And indeed methinks the passions of our mind, are not unlike the four humours of our bodies, whereto, Cicero well compares them in the aforesaid book: for if blood, phlegm, choler, or melancholy exceed the due proportion required to the constitution and health of our bodies, presently we fall into some disease: even so, if the passions of the mind be not moderated according to reason (and that temperature virtue requireth) immediately the soul is molested with some malady. But if the humours be kept in a due proportion they are the preservatives of health, and perhaps, health itself. (1604, sig. B8^v – C1^r)

As Paster and others have demonstrated, the kind of careful moderation advocated by Wright is common in early modern thinking about the passions in general. Although this aspect can be overemphasized – passions were understood by early moderns to have many positive and beneficial effects too – there is no escaping a certain anxiety about the consequences of unregulated passions in early modern non-literary and literary writings, including those by Shakespeare. Both for the individual and for society, excessive passions were thought to have detrimental effects on people's health and well-being or to cause general disturbance and discord. This is also implied in another early modern term for the passions: 'perturbations'. As Wright puts it, 'those actions then which are common with us, and beasts, we call Passions and Affections, or perturbations of the mind', and, he continues, '[t]hey are called perturbations for that [...] they trouble wonderfully the soul, corrupting the judgement, & seducing the will, inducing (for the most part) to vice, and commonly withdrawing from virtue, and therefore some call them maladies, or sores of the soul' (1604, sig. B4^r – B4^v). Passions are powerful forces, which quite literally 'perturb' the body and the mind. Moreover, Wright, like his contemporaries, believed that the passions were common to both humans and animals, implying that unless humans deploy their God-given reason to subdue their passions, they may become too animal-like in their behaviour.

These descriptions of the passions, together with the language of the humours, provide helpful context for the lines spoken by Prince Escalus early in *Romeo and Juliet* when he admonishes the Capulets and Montagues for (once again) disturbing the streets of Verona with their relentless fighting:

> Rebellious subjects, enemies to peace,
> Profaners of this neighbour-stained steel –
> Will they not hear? – What ho, you men, you beasts!
> That quench the fire of your pernicious rage
> With purple fountains issuing from your veins:
> On pain of torture, from those bloody hands
> Throw your mistempered weapons to the ground,
> And hear the sentence of your moved prince.
>
> (1.1.72–79)

Propelled by their hot and fiery rage, the two warring families behave just like the excessive passions they embody – like rebellious subjects and enemies to peace – *and* like beasts unregulated by reason. Their weapons too are 'mistempered' – a possible reference to the humoral heat of their passions – while the 'purple fountains' of blood 'issuing from [their] veins' reads like a perverse image of 'blood-letting', the medical practice of 'bleeding' a patient to reduce any humoral excess. Except that, in this case, the 'patients' – the Montagues and the Capulets – seem to be letting blood both from themselves and from each other without any hope of reducing the choleric heat in their blood.

Of the early modern passions, anger was one of the most feared 'perturbations', not least because of its associations with political unrest, as we see in Escalus's speech and as we will see too in Section 3 on *Julius Caesar*. In his examination of the passions in *A Philosophical Discourse entitled The Anatomy of the Mind*, published in 1576, Thomas Rogers begins his chapter on anger with the following definition:

> Anger is defined after two sorts, either according to her nature or according to her effect. Those which expound the nature of it say it is a heat of blood, and inflaming of the same, even to the innermost part of man. According to the effect it is thus defined: Anger is a lust or desire to punish, or to be revenged on him which seemeth to have hurt us [...] [T]he anger of superiors towards their inferiors, that is of magistrates towards wicked violators of the law, is good and profitable for a common well, but when inferior persons are moved with the same against another, then it is both dangerous and damnable: dangerous because that if they should be resisted, it must needs follow that some be hurt or slain, whence rises parttaking, dissention and war: and damnable, because it is against the commandment of God, who willeth us to be in love and charity with all men. (1576, sig. C5^v – C6^r)

Rogers's definition follows the humoral pattern of describing anger as a hot and 'inflaming' passion 'even to the innermost of man', that is, as a passion found inside the body. His remarks provide further context for Escalus's speech. Escalus is angry with the two families, but his anger differs from theirs because it is like that of Rogers's 'magistrates', whose righteous anger against 'violators of the law' is a social necessity. This exemplifies another key point about early modern emotions – one which, in my experience, prompts productive discussion in the classroom – namely that, in the early modern mindset, the supposedly 'medical' discourse of humoral theory is often deeply interwoven with political, moral, and religious discourses, in direct contrast to modern-day attempts to keep these discourses separate.

As I hope this section has shown so far, the language of humoral theory and the related discourses of the passions that we find in early modern sources such as the treatises by Wright and Rogers provide students with a great deal of helpful context for close reading and analysing emotions at work in Shakespeare's plays. Deploying humoralism as a contextual and analytical framework both enhances students' understanding of Shakespeare's emotional vocabulary and helps them historicize that vocabulary. They are encouraged to look at Shakespeare's descriptions of emotion, as it were, with fresh eyes, and what they discover is an emotional experience that is distinctly different from what they might have expected. Moreover, in my experience, students generally enjoy exploring the systematic 'strangeness' of the humours and, not least, the many – to modern ears – bizarre-sounding cures and remedies used to alleviate their excessive production. Many students will have heard of the practice of blood-letting (which was used well beyond the early modern period, right into the nineteenth century), but some of the dietary remedies can be delightful discoveries: one of my favourite examples is the use of rhubarb to cure an attack of choler, which is referenced in John Webster's tragedy *The Duchess of Malfi*. Once students have a fundamental hold on humoral theory and understand some of the medical and cultural discourses attached to it – such as the anxiety about excessive passions – they soon begin to spot moments in Shakespeare's writing where emotional experience is either explicitly or implicitly underwritten by humoral terminology.

Love and Hate in Romeo and Juliet

As we have seen, the explosive heat of anger, fuelled by the humour of yellow bile, was viewed as a powerful and potentially dangerous phenomenon in a number of early modern contexts. Anger is a close cognate of hate, rage, and fury – the emotions that cause much of the violence in *Romeo and Juliet*. The seat in the humoral body of such emotions, or passions, was generally believed to be the liver – hence Hamlet's self-deprecating lament that he is 'pigeon-livered and lack[s] gall' (2.2.512). Meaning that Hamlet's liver is too small and weedy to produce the gall (or yellow bile) that he needs in order to behave like a proper avenger. Here, we also see a common connection between anger and courage, another emotion typically located in the liver.[15] However, the liver was also believed to be the seat of yet another hot and fiery passion: love. As we will see in Section 4, in *The Anatomy of Melancholy*, Robert Burton locates the powerful passion of 'heroical love' in the liver, and in *Twelfth Night*, the Count Orsino describes the love that he feels for Olivia as 'a motion of the liver' (2.4.94). Rogers, in *A Philosophical Discourse entitled The Anatomy of the Mind*, follows his chapter on anger directly with one on love, which he describes as '[t]he greatest and most burning affection' (1576, sig. D1^v). While he acknowledges some of the positive aspects of love, Rogers warns that '[t]he effects of Love are strange, and the very remembrances and reading of them ought to make love to be odious, and more to be shunned than any other Perturbation which men are subject to. For it suffreth the passioned never to be in quiet, but continually tormented' (1576, sig. D3^r). Romeo is a stereotypical tormented lover when we first meet him – very much like Orsino when we first meet him in *Twelfth Night* – but love works on several levels in *Romeo and Juliet*. It is not just the emotion that defines Romeo as a character or that defines the relationship between him and Juliet, it also works as a humorally-inspired force within the play's overheated emotional environment – quite similarly to hate. Friar Lawrence helps the two young lovers, but he also functions as the voice of moderation in respect of their emotions. When he agrees to marry them in secret, he prefaces the ceremony with a prophetic warning:

> These violent delights have violent ends,
> And in their triumph die like fire and powder,
> Which as they kiss consume. The sweetest honey
> Is loathsome in his own deliciousness,
> And in the taste confounds the appetite.
> Therefore love moderately, long love doth so;
> Too swift arrives as tardy as too slow.
>
> (2.6.9–15)

---

[15] For an in-depth analysis of Hamlet's lines in the context of humoralism, see Paster, 2004, pp. 47–50.

The Friar's speech rather contradicts the idea that the love between Romeo and Juliet is simply the antithesis of their families' hatred. When students are familiar with the fiery language associated with anger and hate, both in *Romeo and Juliet* and elsewhere in Shakespeare's plays, they will note that the Friar's description indicates that love – if it is too 'hot', too much like 'fire and gunpowder' and too rash and hasty – may come to, or bring about, a violent end. The Friar's voice is not the only one in the play to warn against overheated love. The Nurse, albeit in a much more comical vein, chides Juliet for being too 'hot' when the latter impatiently chivvies her messenger: 'O God's lay, dear, / Are you so hot?' (2.5.60–61). Whether sombre or comical, these remarks suggest that the two young protagonists' feelings are somehow part and parcel of an emotional environment that is generally far too hot.

Moreover, there is a certain correspondence in the play between the hot and fiery emotions – both love and hate – that are felt by the inhabitants of Verona and the actual temperature in their streets and buildings. At the Capulet party in act one, situations involving love and hate follow each other in quick succession. Romeo sees Juliet and is attracted by her torch-like brightness. Tybalt hears Romeo speak and feels his own flesh tremble with a combination of enforced 'patience' and 'wilful choler' (1.5.88). Yet even before these fiery emotions erupt, the physical environment of the party has become overheated, as we learn in old Capulet's instructions to his servants to 'quench the fire, the room is grown too hot' (1.5.27). A similar correspondence between emotion and environment is expressed more explicitly in act three, when Benvolio – before the fateful fight between Mercutio, Tybalt, and eventually Romeo – is painfully aware of the dangerous effects of a hot day on the humoral temperaments of his companions:

> I pray thee, good Mercutio, let's retire:
> The day is hot, the Capels are abroad,
> And if we meet we shall not scape a brawl,
> For now, these hot days, is the mad blood stirring.
>
> (3.1.1–4)

Rather than reading these examples of hot environments and hot emotions metaphorically or symbolically, students may instead be encouraged to read them in the context of what Paster has described as a reciprocal relation between the humoral body and its surroundings – what she terms the early modern 'ecology of the passions' (2004, p. 28).[16] As Paster explains, the humoral body was not understood as sealed off from its surroundings; rather, thanks to its humoral makeup, it had a certain porous quality, which makes sense when we remember that the four humours in the body were related to the four elements of air, fire, water, and earth. The humoral body and its emotions were thought to be affected by external phenomena such as hot weather, but the relationship was reciprocal in the sense that emotionally heated bodies might simultaneously affect their surroundings. Or, as Paster puts it, early modern humoralism 'recognizes the influence of environment on the passions and the effect of human passions on the objective world outside self' (2004, p. 42).[17] The key point here, then, is to encourage students to see how this material reciprocity between emotion and environment differs from a symbolic relationship where, say, descriptions of nature are made to reflect or mirror human feelings – a device more often found in nineteenth-century and Romantic literature than in that of the early modern period. In other words, when reading the language of 'heat' in *Romeo and Juliet*, students may be encouraged to imagine 'heat' in humoral terms and to look for the hot emotions that inhabit both the bodies of the characters in the play and their environments.

Finally, there is another aspect to humoral theory that matters greatly to the kind of reading I am encouraging in this section – and that is to do with the often explicitly gendered discourse of this supposedly 'medical' knowledge system. The young male characters in *Romeo and Juliet* – on both sides of the feud – behave entirely predictably according to humoralism, because men, and especially young men, were thought to be hotter and

---

[16] See also Paster, 2004, chapter 1, and Steggle, 2018, p. 226.

[17] See also Steggle: 'the very distinction between cognition, or how a mind perceives and analyses the world around it, and emotion, which entails a body and mind directly affected by their environment, is itself much hazier in the context of a humoral understanding of consciousness' (2018, p. 226).

drier than women, which made them more inclined to both choler and courage. Nicholas Coeffeteau, in *A Table of Human Passions* (translated from French into English in 1621), writes that 'young men, and such as have their blood hot and boiling, are wonderfully ready to commit insolencies' (1621, sig. 2B8^r), while Thomas Wright affirms that 'young men's incontinency, boldness, and confidence proceedeth of heat which aboundeth in them, and those, whose complexions are hottest, are most subject to these affections' (1604, sig. D3^v). It may sound as if these texts are seeking to put a moral dampener on the excessive heat of young men's bodies – and this is certainly part of their discourse – but early modern emotion theorists both warn against male heat and celebrate it too, especially when comparing it to women's supposedly colder and weaker bodies. As Paster points out, early modern humoralism was no neutral knowledge system; it was inherently misogynistic, reflecting much of the gendered prejudice of the time.[18] Women, because lacking in heat, were also believed to lack courage – indeed, the 'boldness and confidence' that Wright talks of – and so were inevitably placed in an emotionally inferior position in respect of men.

When taking this aspect of humoralism into account in classroom readings and discussions of *Romeo and Juliet*, I would ask students to consider what Shakespeare does with it in the play. While he ostensibly follows a relatively straightforward humoral pattern in the aggressive behaviour of the young Capulet and Montague males with their boiling blood and readiness to 'commit insolencies', something else happens when we look more closely at Romeo and Juliet themselves. Why might it be that the language used by others to describe Juliet – and the language that she uses herself – often contains references to heat and fire? Does she in fact have as much courageous 'heat' in her as the men around her? Her ability to suppress her fears when accepting the Friar's potion might suggest as much. In other words, might students want to ask if and how Juliet subverts the stereotypical humoral perception of women as lacking both heat and 'boldness'? Romeo, on the other hand, has a great deal of heat in his humoral makeup too – when he attacks Tybalt in revenge for Mercutio's death, he summons 'fire-eyed fury' (3.1.115) – but when he is banished, his

---

[18] See Paster, 1998, p. 430.

tears are described by the Friar as 'womanish' (3.3.110). While this is in itself a predictably misogynistic remark, Romeo's tearful reaction might also suggest a gendered emotionality that is both literally and conceptually fluid. In other words, when students look closely into the text, they may find that Shakespeare sometimes departs from, or inverts, some of humoralism's stereotypes, playing instead with humoral idioms to create an even more complex and less predictable dramatization of emotion.

Early Modern Humoral Theory: A Learning Activity

This activity works well as preparation for the following two activities, both of which rely on students having acquired a fundamental knowledge and understanding of humoral theory. Learning the system of humoral theory is not unlike learning a grammatical system, but I would seek to avoid a passive learning experience in which students mainly receive information rather than actively acquiring it. Moreover, it is useful for students to experience the slight variations between the versions of humoral theory that they will encounter, both in primary texts from the early modern period and in contemporary criticism, so that they understand that there is not a single authoritative version. In addition to the secondary readings that I have listed in this section, students will find a great deal of information online. I have listed two references to resources available from the Folger Shakespeare Library, and the US National Library of Medicine offers a helpful and visually inviting online exhibition on Shakespeare and humoral theory ('"And there's the humor of it!" Shakespeare and the Four Humors'), which was guest-curated by Gail Kern Paster and Theodore M. Brown and refreshed in 2022. The exhibition and the Folger resources are an excellent place for students to start to gather information about humoral theory. For this activity, I would ask small groups of students to work together, exploring these resources and mining them for information – and supplementing their findings by referring to the critical texts listed in this section. Students should then write a short account of early modern humoral theory, using their own words. Prompts to guide their writing might be:

(1) Describe the properties (hot/cold/dry/wet) of each of the four humours and their connection to the elements, seasons, planets, human age span, as well as their location in the body

(2) Provide examples of how the humours might affect the body
(3) Discuss how the humours were thought to relate to gender
(4) Are the humours the same as what we call 'emotions' – why/why not?

Reading the Language of Heat in Shakespeare's Verona: Two Learning Activities

(1) **Heat, fire, love and hate in Romeo and Juliet.** This activity seeks to enhance students' understanding of the close relationship between love and hate in the play by asking them to identify as many references to heat, fire, and fieriness as they can find in the text. In other words, the activity works well either as a set task for students when they read the play in advance of a teaching session, or it may be adapted to a set group task during teaching, where students may help each other 'scan' the text for references. If students are not reading the whole play, I would provide them with selected passages (the ones cited in this section). The second part of the activity described in the following, where students reflect on the findings, could be done as a teacher-led discussion or set as a writing task.

Instructions

When students have assembled a substantial number of references to 'heat' in the play (there are many), they should be asked to look at them closely in order to determine their relationship with descriptions or expressions of either love or hate or both. The aim is for students to (1) discover how the language of heat is frequently employed to describe the nature and effects of both love and hate (often referring to both emotions at the same time), and (2) to reflect on what this means at a discursive level in the play – that is, students should be asked to reflect on what happens to our interpretation of *Romeo and Juliet* when the two key emotions in the play – love and hate – turn out not to be simply antithetical but also interchangeable. In order to reflect on this question from a historically informed perspective, students should simultaneously deploy their knowledge about humoral theory and about early modern understanding of excessive passions as needing regulation and moderation as a contextual framework.

(2) **Choleric masculinity** and the emotional environment of heat. This activity asks students to (1) close read and compare two scenes from *Romeo and Juliet* where violence and male behaviour take place in a humorally inspired environment of heat and anger, and (2) to search early modern source texts on the passions for relevant contextual knowledge. The first of the two scenes is the opening scene of the play, which begins with a punning exchange between the two Capulet servants, Sampson and Gregory, and eventually escalates into a full-on street fight between the Capulets and Montagues until interrupted by Prince Escalus (1.1.1 to 1.1.72). The second is the scene cited earlier in this section, where Benvolio's opening lines (3.1.1) establish an intrinsic connection between the literally hot environment of the Veronese summer and the danger of a violent encounter with the Capulets.

Instructions

Questions to ask students to help guide and facilitate their reading may include:

(1) How does Shakespeare build an atmosphere of tension and aggression through the dialogue?
(2) Bearing in mind the historical context of humoral theory, how should we read any references to choler, heat, or fire in these scenes?
(3) Bearing in mind the historical context of humoral theory, how does Shakespeare deploy humoral ideas about masculinity – especially the emotional behaviours of young men – in these scenes?

Both scenes gradually build tension and aggression via witty exchanges and puns – eventually substituting swords for words – and both scenes use references to choler, heat, and humoral masculinity to signal a certain behavioural pattern. The descriptions by Nicholas Coeffeteau and Thomas Wright, which I cited earlier in this section, of young men's 'boiling blood', their boldness and confidence, and their readiness to behave with insolence, provide a helpful context for this activity, and students may be encouraged to search these and other early modern sources for additional descriptions of 'choleric masculinity'. By using the helpful and freely available bibliographical list of 'Sources of Early Modern Emotion in English, 1500-1700' (earlymodernemotion.net), students will be able to find relevant sources for 'anger, choler, rage, fury, wrath and ire' and proceed to explore texts of their choice by using the online search function on the free resources: 'Early English Books Online Collections' by the University of Michigan Library (https://quod.lib.umich.edu/e/eebogroup/) or 'EarlyPrint: Curating and Exploring Early Printed English' by Northwestern University and Washington University in St. Louis (https://earlyprint.org/), or on EEBO, if available. These resources will allow students to search for terms such as 'anger' or 'fury' and 'heat' and to experiment with different search word combinations. A key aim of this part of the activity is to facilitate student training in how to use online databases and their search engines for research purposes by actively engaging with their interfaces and functions. I would suggest letting students take on this activity in small groups, so that they can divide searches between them and share discoveries. As I have tried to demonstrate in this section, engaging with early modern primary texts written specifically about the passions significantly helps to contextualize and historicize close readings of emotion-centred situations and dialogue in Shakespeare's plays. Again, using these sources can be challenging for students, not only because they require time and persistence but also because they can frustrate expectations of finding straightforward answers. It is often necessary to acknowledge these challenges, but it is also possible to engage students in a positive conversation about why historical material might evade the questions we ask of it – for example, because the mindset that produced these texts is at a historical remove from us. If students can be encouraged to appreciate this unfamiliar mindset, I believe they will also find the task more rewarding.

As a part of this activity, students may do some further work on the gendered perception of 'hot' and 'cold' humours, which I have discussed earlier in this section. They may be asked to look closely at the ways in which the two protagonists of the play both embody and subvert humoral stereotypes. They may be asked to investigate questions about Juliet's humoral qualities – reflecting on why she embodies humorally 'hot' qualities when, as a female character, she might be expected to be made of 'cooler' stuff. Students may also be asked to look at Romeo's humoral qualities, comparing him with Tybalt's very explicit humoral 'heat', for example, and reflect on his different and changeable emotional patterns in the second half of the play, from 'hot-headed' anger at Tybalt over Mercutio's death to tears at his own banishment. Finally, drawing on their answers to these questions, students may be asked to reflect on the ways in which Shakespeare deploys the humoral theory knowledge system in the play – does he ever depart from, or challenge, humoral ideas? If yes, what might this tell us about the contribution of drama and literature towards ideas about emotions? Do literary texts also create, or shape, a given culture's understanding of what emotions are and do?

Background Reading and Online Resources

Escolme, Bridget. (2014). *Emotional Excess on the Shakespearean Stage* (esp. 'Introduction and Chapter 3), London: Arden Shakespeare.

Paster, Gail Kern. (2004). *Humoring the Body: Emotions and the Shakespearean Stage* (esp. 'Introduction' and Chapter 1), Chicago: Chicago University Press.

French, Esther. (2016). Balancing the body and consulting the heavens: Medicine in Shakespeare's time'. The Folger Shakespeare Library. www.folger.edu/blogs/shakespeare-and-beyond/elizabethan-medicine-shakespeare/

Kambaskovic, Danijela. (2017). 'Humoral Theory'. In Susan Broomhall, ed., *Early Modern Emotions: An Introduction*, London: Routledge, pp. 39–42.

Lyon, Karen. (2015). 'The Four Humors: Eating in the Renaissance'. The Folger Shakespeare Library. www.folger.edu/blogs/shakespeare-and-beyond/the-four-humors-eating-in-the-renaissance/

Steggle, Matthew. (2018). 'The Humours in Humour: Shakespeare and Early Modern Psychology'. In Heather Hirschfeld (ed.), *The Oxford handbook of Shakespearean Comedy*, Oxford, Oxford University Press, pp. 220–235.

US National Library of Medicine. (2012–2022-present). '"And there's the humor of it!": Shakespeare and the Four Humors' (online exhibition). www.nlm.nih.gov/exhibition/shakespeare-and-the-four-humors/index.html

3 Emotion, Motion and Commotion in *Julius Caesar*

The purpose of this section is to suggest ways in which to teach *Julius Caesar* by exploring early modern emotions as closely related to ideas of *movement*. As I noted in the introduction, emotion historians frequently study the etymological history of 'emotion words' in order to uncover the ways in which their meaning changes over time. In this section, I will discuss the history of the word 'emotion' itself, showing that Shakespeare's understanding of emotion would have involved some semantic overlaps with 'motion' and 'commotion'. In Shakespeare's plays, emotions often function as forces that set characters and events in 'motion', or create 'commotion', and this dramatic pattern, I will show, is in fact closely related to Shakespeare's understanding of what emotions *are*.

I will argue that the teaching methods and learning activities informed by this historicist approach will enhance students' understanding of *Julius Caesar* in two key ways: (1) students will understand the ways in which the play explores a distinct early modern understanding of emotions as moving and moveable forces – an understanding which is also underwritten by Shakespeare's indebtedness to classical rhetoric and which differs significantly from modern understandings of emotions as individual, subjective and internal feelings – and (2) by drawing on the idea of motion and commotion as embedded in the early modern understanding of emotion, students will be able to re-imagine the early modern theatre space as an emotional space full of movement, both onstage and in the auditorium. This section thus offers a contextual and analytical framework and a set of four learning activities which will support students both in performing contextualized literary analysis of *Julius Caesar* and in exploring aspects of early modern theatre history.

Other plays which might be taught by drawing on the framework outlined in this section include *Titus Andronicus* and *Coriolanus*, but the understanding of early modern emotions as moving and moveable forces is widely applicable across the whole Shakespeare canon. The contents of this section – both the introductory contextual discussion and the suggested learning activities – may be adapted to suit different teaching formats and learning levels. Teachers may wish to draw on the section for a teaching format involving a lecture and seminar combination, for example, or for a longer seminar-based format. The instructions for the four learning activities may be given as instructions to students working either individually or in pairs or groups, and combined with plenum discussion, student presentations, and small written assignments. Finally, like the other sections in the Element, this section includes a selection of helpful critical background texts which may be included in a course pack or given to students as instructions for preparation before the class.

Emotions in Julius Caesar

We may not tend to think of *Julius Caesar* as a play about emotion so much as a play about politics. Dramatizing as it does a key moment in Roman history – the assassination of Julius Caesar in 44 BCE – the play asks complicated questions about the relationship of ethics and power and is frequently deployed as a literary vehicle through which to address modern political dilemmas too. However, as Matthew Steggle has observed, although 'it is generally accepted that *Julius Caesar* explores the theatricality of politics[,] one might also add that a central element of this is the display, the reading, the moving of, and the ability to appear to be responding to, signs of external emotion in others' (2007, p. 134). At the centre of the play is Mark Antony's famous funeral oration for the assassinated Caesar, which has an electrifying effect on the emotions of the Roman crowd. Following Antony's stirring speech, the Romans set off to avenge Caesar, and their collective anger soon claims its first and entirely accidental victim. Encountering the poet Cinna in the street, the angry mob attacks him, tearing him limb from limb, because his name is Cinna – a name he unfortunately shares with one of Caesar's assassins:

> CINNA THE POET I am not Cinna the conspirator.
> 4 PLEBIAN It is no matter, his name's Cinna. Pluck but his name out of his heart and turn him going.
>
> 3 PLEBIAN Tear him, tear him! Come, brands ho! firebrands! To Brutus', to Cassius', burn all! Some to Decius' house, and some to Casca's, some to Ligarius'! Away, go!

(3.3.29–34)

The scene is short but horrific. It dramatizes crowd emotion at its worst and most violent and showcases Shakespeare's ability to imagine such emotion in action. It also implies a powerful, and in this case dangerous, connection between emotion and motion. Having been 'moved' – emotionally speaking – by Antony to feel pity for Caesar and anger at his assassins, the Romans channel their emotion into outward and forward movement as they charge through the streets of Rome.

As I explained in Section 1, the word 'emotion' did not mean quite the same thing to Shakespeare and his contemporaries as it does to us today. We typically use 'emotion' as an umbrella term for a wide range of feelings such as love, anger, fear, or happiness, as well as for more 'fuzzy' feelings such as anxiety, curiosity, or irritation. Even if we disagree on how such feelings should be understood – as biological or as culturally determined processes – we still tend to agree on using 'emotions' as a suitable term for them. When Shakespeare was writing, however, feelings such as love or anger were more frequently known as 'passions', as we also saw in Section 1. 'Emotion', by contrast, was only just beginning to enter the English language – in fact, according to entries in the *Oxford English Dictionary*, its first usages coincide with the beginning of Shakespeare's writing career in the 1590s. Moreover, in the sixteenth and seventeenth centuries, 'emotion' could still carry meanings close to its etymological root, such as 'movement, disturbance or unrest', or even 'political agitation, civil unrest; a public commotion or uprising' (*OED* 1a and 1b).[19] When Antony 'moves' the Roman crowd, then, we may re-imagine emotion and motion as being intrinsically connected.

An additional closely related word that helps to understand how Shakespeare dramatizes crowd emotion in *Julius Caesar* would be 'commotion'. When Shakespeare was writing, 'commotion', like today, could mean a 'public disturbance or disorder' (*OED* 4a), but the word also carried meanings which are no longer in use. One definition of commotion, which fell out of use in the mid eighteenth century, but which would have been

---

[19] Scholars of early modern emotion routinely note this etymological history. See Paster, Rowe, and Floyd-Wilson, 2004; Escolme, 2014; and Craik, 2020.

familiar to Shakespeare and his contemporaries, was 'mental perturbation, agitation, excitement' (*OED* 5). Among the examples given by the *OED* for this now obsolete definition is a quotation from Shakespeare's *Troilus and Cressida*: 'Kingdom[e]d Achilles in commotion rages'. Here, the great Homeric hero's anger, with which the *Iliad* famously begins, is imagined as a kind of mental 'commotion', or indeed what we today would call emotion. We find another example in Shakespeare and John Fletcher's *Henry VIII*, where the Duke of Norfolk, observing the emotional body language of Cardinal Wolsey, surmises that '[s]ome strange commotion / Is in his brain' (3.2.112–113). In both these examples, commotion conveys the emotionally stirred state of an individual, but as its prefix suggests, commotion may also express the collective emotion of a group. The crowds in *Julius Caesar* certainly share feelings of anger, rage, and fury, and driven by these feelings, they 'move together' as one collective body. Etymology and semantics can, then, I suggest, be useful tools for thinking about emotions historically and thus for teaching Shakespeare's emotions. We may no longer directly connect 'emotion', 'motion', and 'commotion' in our vocabulary or our imagination, but there is evidence that Shakespeare and his contemporaries did, and so paying attention to such connections offers a historicist framework for analysing emotions at work in a play such as *Julius Caesar*.

Feelings in Motion

When seeking to understand early modern passions both ontologically and practically – that is, both what the passions are and what they do – 'motion' is a good place to start. To an early modern emotion theorist such as Thomas Wright, the process of experiencing emotions or passions is also the experience of certain kinds of motion. In *The Passions of the Mind in General*, Wright refers to the passions as 'motions of the soul' (1604, sig. B4^v), and he generally relies on a systematic, step-by-step account of how the passions operate. First, the passions are moved by some external object, which is perceived through the senses – sight, hearing, and so on – or by an imagined or remembered event. When the passions are stirred, they produce an effect on the body: they change it, moving it from the inside.

Or as Wright asserts: 'when these affections are stirring in our minds they alter the humours of our bodies, causing some passion or alteration in them' (1604, sig. B4^v). The experience of feeling angry might, to the early modern imagination, involve the following motions: first, the perception or imagining of some provocation to anger and, next, the blood rushing towards the heart and overheating it. After these might follow outward signs of anger, such as a contortion of the face as well as anger-fuelled action (or motion) in the form of violence against others. This forest-fire-like process might be quenched in time by the summoning of reason, but once it is set in motion, it is difficult to stop – as indeed we see in *Julius Caesar*, when the incensed crowds rush through the city, killing and burning as they go.

In *Julius Caesar*, the key vehicle for moving the passions is rhetoric. The anger of the crowd is provoked by Antony's words and by his carefully calculated actions. During the funeral speech, he shows Caesar's bloodied mantle to the crowd and, next, Caesar's corpse with its multiple stab wounds. The effect of his oratorical skill is anticipated by his antagonists. When Brutus grants Antony permission to speak at Caesar's funeral, Cassius warns him: 'Know you how much the people may be moved / By that which he will utter' (3.1.233–34). Classical rhetoric was an essential part of the humanist education that Shakespeare received – if, as is generally believed, he attended the grammar school in Stratford-upon-Avon – and scholars, including Lynn Enterline, have demonstrated the profound effect of rhetoric on Shakespeare's mind and professional career.[20]

Moreover, it is important to note that to Shakespeare, rhetoric would have provided not only a system or a manual for producing emotionally stirring speech but also essential knowledge about what the passions are and what they do. As Benedict Robinson has argued, rhetoric to early moderns 'contained the most extensively particularized discourse on the passions, offering principles for moving the passions of others in concrete social

---

[20] See Enterline, 2012.

scenes' (2021, p. 3).[21] So it is not surprising that Wright in *The Passions of the Mind in General* turns to rhetoric in order to explain why and how the passions are set in motion. In book five of his treatise, Wright offers a striking comparison of the continuous motion of the passions with that of urban waterways. In the city, Wright explains, water moves in three distinct ways: 'by fountains or springs, by rivers or conduits, or by rain, snow or hailstones'. In the same way, says Wright, the passions are moved in three different ways: 'by humours arising in our bodies, by external senses and secret passage of sensual objects [and] by the descent or commandment of reason' (1604, sig. L3^r). That is, the passions arise like fountains, they move like rivers, and they are subdued by the descent of reason like rain from the sky.

When explaining how the passions are moved through the sensory perception of some external object, Wright also refers to a common device in forensic rhetoric which involves showing a physical object so as to underline an important point of one's speech: 'To persuade any matter we intend, or to stir up any passion in a multitude, if we can aptly confirm our opinion or intention with any visible object, no doubt the persuasion would be more forcible and the passion more potent' (1604, sig. L6^v). Which is precisely what Antony does when he shows Caesar's mantle and Caesar's corpse to the Roman crowds.[22] Further on, Wright also cites the rhetorical commonplace that an orator who wishes to move others must first be moved himself, which will enable him to express his emotion through action: 'Therefore if we intend to imprint a passion in another, it is requisite first it be stamped in our hearts: for through our voices, eyes and gestures the world will [...] thoroughly perceive how we are affected' (1604, sig. M7^v). The effects of this advice are again manifest in *Julius Caesar*, when Antony

---

[21] See also Enterline 2012; Robinson 2020; and Rhodes, 2020.

[22] One of the most studied classical textbooks on rhetoric in early modern England was Quintilian's *Institutio Oratoria* (Institutes of Oratory) (c. 95 CE). Both Wright and Shakespeare may easily have been familiar with the example used by Quintilian to describe how physical objects move listeners: 'The blood-stained toga of Julius Caesar, when exhibited in the forum, excited the populace of Rome almost to madness' (2006, 6.1.30–31).

shows signs of his emotion to the Roman crowd, and when they, perceiving his emotion, begin to share it.

Rhetoric, then, with its emphasis on moving the passions of others, provided early moderns with an account of emotions as highly dynamic processes. Early modern passions by this account were moving and moveable forces and, as Robinson argues, need to be understood as 'a fundamentally social phenomenon' (2020, p. 218). This is somewhat different from modern accounts of emotions as subjective, individual feelings. Modern emotions are typically something we 'have' or experience as individuals rather than something we immediately share. To be sure, shared or collective emotion is a modern phenomenon too, and students will no doubt be able to think of examples to compare with the collective emotional behaviour in *Julius Caesar*. I would certainly encourage such comparative thinking in the classroom, but I would also encourage students to explore the ways in which the early modern understanding of emotion as a dynamic social encounter is nonetheless a distinct and historically situated understanding of what it means to 'feel things'.

Analysing Emotion in Julius Caesar: *Two Learning Activities*

(1) **Responding to Antony's funeral oration.** The first of the following two suggested activities – both of which involve classroom close reading and literary analysis – seeks to focus students' attention on the emotional effects that Antony's funeral oration has on his listeners. When reading the speech, students should be asked to pay attention to the responses of the Roman crowd and to the emotions these responses convey. While the activity focuses on the responses to the speech rather than the speech itself, it would also be useful to introduce students to the rhetorical devices used by Antony.[23]

---

[23] For a helpful analysis of the rhetorical structure of the speech, see Rhodes, 2020. Another excellent and free resource on classical rhetoric is 'The Forest of Rhetoric' by Gideon Burton (Brigham Young University): https://rhetoric.byu.edu.

Instructions

Ask students to close read lines 3.2.74 to 3.2.250 (which include Antony's entire speech and the final crowd reactions) either in pairs or small groups. Students should note all the lines spoken by individuals in the crowd and by the crowd in unison, and in so doing, they should try to 'map' the emotional escalation in the crowd by describing the development of the crowd's emotions in their own words. If available, a digital writing board such as 'Padlet' could also be used here, so that students may share notes and quotations in real time. The aim is for students to be able to discern a development from feelings of mild suspicion of Antony, to pity (both for Antony and for Caesar) to intense rage expressed in collective monosyllabic or near-monosyllabic exclamations such as 'Revenge! About! Seek! Burn! Fire! Kill! Slay!' (3.2.199). Students are then asked to imagine this emotional development in terms of movement: are there any specific words both in Antony's speech and in the crowd's reactions which convey or imply movement, both emotional and literal? Here, students might note the high frequency of active verbs such as 'stir', 'rise', 'seek', 'pluck', and 'fetch', for example. They should also be asked to pay attention to the moment when Antony descends from the pulpit and stands among the crowd, which presses against him (lines 160–166). Sensing the physical pressure of the crowd, Antony objects, 'Nay, press not so upon me. Stand far off' (3.2.165). Questions to ask students could include:

(1) How do motion and emotion converge in this moment?
(2) Is Antony showing awareness of the dangerous 'game' he is playing with the crowd's emotions? If so, what are the words that give this away?

Again, the close reading and analysis of these passages may take place in pairs or small groups with students noting down their observations, before a teacher-led discussion where the students are able to share and develop their responses to the activity.

(2) **Framing Antony's funeral speech.** The second activity seeks to draw students' attention to Shakespeare's framing of Antony's speech with two brief but emotionally charged moments: the end of act three, scene one

(lines 254–297) and act three, scene three – the vicious gang-attack on Cinna the poet – which I cited at the beginning of this section. The aim here is to enhance students' understanding of the emotional content of the funeral speech by noting how Shakespeare leads up to it and how he dramatizes its consequences. The aim, moreover, is to train students in the analysis of play texts by paying attention to scenes or passages which might otherwise be overlooked in comparison with scenes that are typically considered 'central' and have attracted a great deal of critical attention, such as indeed Antony's funeral speech. When looking for emotions in Shakespeare's plays in general, students will benefit from observing that emotions do not just belong to 'central' scenes and principal characters but are frequently expressed by minor characters of low social status or by anonymous characters, sometimes in scenes that appear less important or secondary to the main plot. In act five of *The Winter's Tale*, for instance, the reunion of Leontes with his long-lost daughter Perdita is narrated as an off-stage event by an unnamed 'Gentleman', who interlaces his own emotional reactions to the event with his description of the emotions displayed by the main characters. Students should also be encouraged to think about how characters with little or no dialogue might express and convey emotions to the theatre audience in potentially powerful ways through facial expressions or bodily gestures.

Instructions

Students should be asked to close read the end of act three, scene one, where Antony is left alone on stage with Caesar's corpse (lines 254–297). The passage begins with a soliloquy spoken by Antony in which Antony prophesies civil war in Italy. A servant of Octavius enters and begins to deliver a message from his master, but interrupts himself when he sees the body of Caesar: 'He [Octavius] did receive his letters and is coming, / And bid me say to you by word of mouth – / O Caesar!' (3.1.279–281). The servant's spontaneous exclamation – 'O Caesar!' – conveys an emotional reaction set in motion by the sight of the corpse, and this reaction in turn moves Antony, who, seeing the other's grief, notes the contagious effect of emotion: 'Passion, I see, is catching, for mine eyes, / Seeing those beads of sorrow stand in thine, / Begin to water' (3.1.282–285). Here, in the shared experience of grief, one character reacts to another through a kind of kinaesthetic motion. Students are asked to explain in their own words what happens during this moment and then to consider how Antony's discovery – that 'passion is catching' – might connect with similar moments during the funeral speech in the next scene. The aim is that students will be able to discern how this brief exchange between Antony and Octavius' servant shows (1) emotions as forces that move back and forth between the two characters and (2) that this moment of emotional contagion is replicated during Antony's funeral speech, where the mutual perception of grief and tears makes for a dynamic emotional connection between Antony and the crowd. The second short passage that students should be asked to look at as part of this activity is act three, scene three (the attack on Cinna the poet). Students should be asked to consider and explain how this apparently extraneous scene dramatizes the effect of Antony's speech and to draw on semantic crossovers between emotion, motion, and commotion as an analytical framework and critical vocabulary for their explanation. The aim is that students will be able (1) to utilize these semantic crossovers in their analysis of the scene and (2) to observe how the funeral speech is dramaturgically framed by these two emotionally charged moments, which in turn help to explain its emotional content and effect.

Movement and the Audience in the Theatre: Two Learning Activities

Julius Caesar, like all of Shakespeare's plays, is remarkably aware of its audience as a physically present active and reactive crowd. The play opens with a group of Roman commoners walking across the stage, before they are told to go home by two haughty tribunes:

> *Enter* FLAVIUS, MURELLIUS and certain Commoners
> *over the stage.*
> FLAVIUS Hence! home, you idle creatures, get you home!
> Is this a holiday? What, know you not
> (Being mechanical) you ought not to walk

> Upon a labouring day, with the sign
> Of your profession? Speak, what trade are you?
> CARPENTER Why, sir, a carpenter.

(1.1.1–6)

Flavius's rebuke 'Is this is a holiday?' would no doubt have amused any early modern audience members who were indeed taking time off from work to go to the theatre. By populating the stage with actors representing common citizens from the very first scene, the play unsettles the boundaries between stage and auditorium: audience members see themselves reflected in these anonymous but very active figures. As Gail Kern Paster observes, citing this very scene: 'one task of theatre in Shakespeare's time and our own is to build community within the confines of the playhouse for the duration of a performance – an affective community defined as such by the physical sharing of presence, witness and emotions' (2020, p. 94). Furthermore, the Roman commoners at this moment are walking across the stage, creating an impression of crowd movement which connects with the standing, moving crowd in the auditorium of the Globe, especially if the actors playing the commoners actually enter via the auditorium and mount the stage from the position of the groundlings, as it has been suggested might have been the case at the first Globe.[24]

Bruce R. Smith has also argued that we should think of the theatre space of the first Globe in terms of movement, both literal and emotional, both on the stage and in the auditorium, and especially in between the two: 'Movement at the Globe was not just a matter of blocking. Rather, the entire space within the wooden O needs to be imagined as full of movement' (2004, p. 147). Moreover, it is not only the theatres of early modern London that we might imagine in this way – as spaces characterized by dynamic, collective motion – but also the city itself. As Paul Menzer notes, the exponential growth of London in the sixteenth century with a population of around two hundred thousand by the end of the

---

[24] See Paster, 2020. For further discussion of early modern audiences, see Low and Myhill. 2011; Menzer, 2011; Hobgood, 2014; and Pollard, 2020.

century, 'London had, by Shakespeare's age, become a city of crowds' (2011, p. 21). As Menzer further observes, Londoners would have 'crowded outside St Paul's to hear a sermon, gathered on corners to listen to chapmen [pedlars, street sellers], packed in yards to wager on cockfights, lining the Fleet for coronation processions, jammed in an amphitheatre for *Lear* or blood sports [such as bear-baiting]' (2011, p. 21). Given the speedy development of London, Menzer also suggests that to early modern Londoners, not least to those moving in from the countryside and smaller towns, the experience of being in a crowd would have been something of a novelty and possibly producing sensations of fear and wariness (2011, p. 21). This context also means that it may be very appropriate to think of the experience of urban living in early modern London in terms of a thrilling but perhaps also alienating mix of emotion, motion, and commotion. Moving in, sensing and engaging with their immediate surroundings, early modern Londoners could have experienced emotions of both positive and negative kinds – from pleasure and excitement to anxiety and fear.

The following two learning activities aim to support students in exploring this idea, and in so doing, to enhance students' understanding of the relationship between the Shakespearean text and the experience of going to the theatre in early modern London. Specifically, the first activity aims (1) to equip students with a method for researching and reimagining the material structures that influenced sensory and emotional experience in the past and (2) to encourage students to think of locations of the past, and the experience of living in them, in dynamic terms such as emotion, motion, and commotion. The second activity aims to enhance students' understanding of the interplay between Shakespeare's text and the theatre audience, and especially of the way in which the text engages theatre audiences in a complex 'conversation' about theatre and emotions through meta-theatrical content. By concentrating on the close reading of a select passage from *Julius Caesar*, students should be able to understand and discuss a key feature of Shakespearean theatre, namely that its intended emotional impact on the audience is not simply 'direct' in the sense that Shakespeare's audiences are encouraged to feel or identify with the emotions represented on the stage. Rather, what we might call the emotional contract between the stage and the auditorium is often 'interrupted' or mediated in the sense that audiences are invited to observe and assess their own emotions in the meta-theatrical comments in Shakespeare's dialogue. As I will explain, the passage from *Julius Caesar* is Casca's narration of an off-stage event where a Roman crowd is represented, not very flatteringly, as reacting emotionally to a political spectacle orchestrated by Caesar and Antony, which in turn invites the audience in the theatre auditorium, who are listening to this account, to look at their own emotional reactions with heightened self-awareness.

(1) **Arriving in the theatre.** This first activity draws inspiration from a key critical question asked by historians of emotion, which I also cited in the introduction to this Element, namely 'what [was it] like to *be* in the past [. . .], what did it *feel* like' (Boddice, 2023, p.10). As Tiffany Stern observes, in early modern London, there were only two ways of crossing the Thames to go to the South Bank theatres, including the first Globe (2004, p. 7). One option was to go by boat, which was the choice of Thomas Platter, a Swiss medical student visiting London in 1599 and one of the few first-hand witnesses of theatre performance in early modern London. Platter's oft-cited account of his theatre experience describes how he crossed the river and 'in the straw-thatched house [. . .] saw the tragedy of the first Emperor Julius Caesar, very pleasing performed'.[25] The other and probably less pleasant option was to go via London Bridge, the only bridge across the Thames in the sixteenth and seventeenth centuries. This might seem easier and quicker than taking a boat, but all the way across the bridge, there were houses with shops on the ground floor, and considering the number of people, animals, and carts that would use it every day, it may well have been one of the busiest and noisiest places in the city. In his *Survey of London*, John Stow remarks that it 'seemeth rather a continual street than a bridge' (1633, sig. D3^v). As Stern further notes, audiences crossing London Bridge to go to the South Bank would have noticed a macabre feature as they arrived at the end of the bridge. On top of the gatehouse were several heads

---

[25] The extract from Platter's diary which describes the performance of *Julius Caesar* is cited in Daniell, 1998, p. 12.

of executed 'traitors' impaled on spikes (2004, pp. 8–9). These are also clearly visible in some Claes Van Visscher's 'Panorama of London' (1616). Using the online file of Visscher's 'Panorama', students may zoom in (e.g., to view the severed heads on the gatehouse in the right foreground) and out to get a sense of the city's layout and the river dividing it in two.

Instructions

Students should be asked to imagine the route taken by someone going to the theatre in early modern London, crossing the Thames either by boat or via London Bridge to go to the Globe on the South Bank, as a journey characterized by emotion, motion, and commotion. Taking inspiration from Thomas Platter's description of his visit to the Globe in 1599, students might be asked to produce a short piece of creative writing assuming the narrative voice of a tourist visiting London and, like Platter, going to see *Julius Caesar* at the Globe. Students should be supplied both with the relevant extract from Platter's diary and with information about London Bridge and the location of the theatres on the South Bank. As noted, they may look at Claes Van Visscher's *Panorama of London* (1616). They may also benefit from exploring early modern London through two excellent resources: the interactive online 'The Map of Early Modern London' (MoEML) and *Shakespeare's Stages* – a multimedia introduction to playing spaces in early modern London (Cambridge University Press). In the writing assignment, students should decide whether to cross the river by boat or bridge, and in either case describe what their early modern tourist narrator might see, hear, and *feel* as they make their way towards the theatre (the commotion both on the water and on the bridge, the heads on spikes, etc.). From the bridge or the riverbank, students may be asked to imagine making their way to and entering the Globe or another of the Bankside theatres. Students may be encouraged to explore the spatial features of the early modern theatre by looking at the well-known drawing of the Swan by Johannes de Witt (1596); however, they should also be asked to focus on the transition from the street to the theatre space, thinking about how the experience of emotion, motion and commotion might extend from the street into the auditorium and then, with reference to the opening scene of *Julius Caesar*, reflecting on Shakespeare's exploration of this emotional interconnection between theatre and urban space.

(2) Meta-theatre and the audience in *Julius Caesar*

This second activity asks students to close read and analyse the representation of the theatre audience within the play. In act one, scene two of *Julius Caesar*, a dialogue takes place between Cassius, Brutus, and Casca in which Casca relates an important off-stage event. We learn that Caesar has been offered the crown three times in the marketplace before the people, each time refusing it. Casca paints a particularly detailed – and contemptuous – image of the Roman crowds and their reactions to the spectacle: 'as [Caesar] refused [the crown] the rabblement hooted, and clapped their chopped hands, and threw up their sweaty nightcaps, and uttered such a deal of stinking breath' (1.2.242–245), and later, 'if the tag-rag people did not clap him and hiss him according as he pleased and displeased them, as they use to do the players in the theatre, I am no true man' (1.2.257–260). The theatre audience at the Globe, listening to this account, could hardly fail to hear themselves depicted in this meta-theatrical commentary, creating a provocative connection between Caesar, the unstable Roman crowd, and themselves. An important function of this provocation seems to be to offer audiences an image of crowd behaviour which is not very flattering, but which heightens their awareness of their own presence, and their possible behaviour, within the theatre space. Importantly, it also heightens their awareness of how emotions within the auditorium might be manipulated by a skilful actor in Casca's continued description of the crowd as strongly susceptible to what he perceives as Caesar's manipulative use of his 'falling sickness' and appeals to the crowd: 'Three or four wenches where I stood cried, "Alas, good soul", and forgave him with all their hearts. But there's no need to be taken of them: if Caesar had stabbed their mothers, they would have done no less' (1.2.270–274). This image of an off-stage crowd, easily swayed by Caesar's histrionics, anticipates the onstage representation of a crowd being incited by Antony's more sophisticated manipulation later in the play, but Casca's description might also alert crowds in the auditorium to the fact that *their* emotions might be manipulated within a theatrical framework that repeatedly draws attention to itself.

Instructions

When analysing this passage, students should first be asked to pay attention to, and to comment on, Casca's description of the Roman crowd. The close reading may take place in pairs or small groups or be set as a reading task or small written assignment in preparation for the teaching session. Ask students to try to identify the meta-theatrical comments in the passage – that is, any content that seems to invite the theatre audience to see themselves mirrored within the dialogue. Students should look closely at the terms used by Casca, such as 'rabblement' and 'tag-rag people', as well as his description of the behaviours of the crowd: they hoot, they clap, they throw their 'sweaty nightcaps' up in the air, and they cry with pity when Caesar swoons. They should then be asked to formulate a 'theory' about the possible effect of these descriptions on the *real* theatre audience watching the scene and listening to Casca's account. Questions to prompt and help students here could include:

(1) Might Shakespeare's audiences be embarrassed, amused, or angry when listening to this not very flattering image of themselves?
(2) What does the passage tell us about the interplay between the stage and the auditorium in Shakespeare's theatre?
(3) How does Casca's description of Caesar's manipulation of the crowd's emotions relate to other scenes of emotional manipulation in *Julius Caesar* (Antony's funeral oration being the obvious example)?
(4) What sort of comment might Shakespeare be making on how emotions work in the theatre?

Background Reading

Hobgood, Allison P. (2014). *Passionate Playgoing in Early Modern England* ('Introduction', pp. 1–33), Cambridge: Cambridge University Press.

McCarthy, Harry, in collaboration with Judy Bae. (2025). *Shakespeare's Stages*, Cambridge: Cambridge University Press

Menzer, Paul. (2011). 'Crowd Control'. In Jennifer A. Low and Nova Myhill, eds., *Imagining the Audience in Early Modern Drama, 1558–1642*, New York: Palgrave Macmillan, pp. 19–36.

Paster, Gail Kern. (2020). 'Communities: *Julius Caesar*'. In Katharine Craik, ed., *Shakespeare and Emotion*, Cambridge: Cambridge University Press, pp. 94–108

Pollard, Tanya. (2020). 'Audiences: *Much Ado About Nothing*, *Measure for Measure*'. In Katharine Craik, ed., *Shakespeare and Emotion*, Cambridge: Cambridge University Press, pp. 109–121.

Rhodes, Neil. (2020). 'Rhetoric: *Titus Andronicus*, *Julius Caesar*'. In Katharine Craik, ed., *Shakespeare and Emotion*, Cambridge: Cambridge University Press, pp. 19–33.

Smith, Bruce. (2004). 'E/loco/com/motion'. In Peter Holland and Stephen Orgel, eds. *From Script to Stage in Early Modern England*, New York: Palgrave, pp. 131–150.

Stern, Tiffany. (2004). *Making Shakespeare: From Stage to Page* (Chapter 2, pp. 7–27), London: Routledge.

4 Melancholy in *Twelfth Night*

In *Twelfth Night*, when the disguised Viola tries to convince the Count Orsino that women are capable of feeling love as strongly as men, she describes the fate of her 'sister', who, like the count himself, has been a victim of unrequited love:

> She never told her love,
> But let concealment like a worm i'th'bud
> Feed on her damask cheek. She pined in thought,
> And with a green and yellow melancholy
> She sat like Patience on a monument,
> Smiling at grief. Was not this love indeed?
>
> (2.4.106–11)

The 'sister' is of course Viola herself, or an imagined vision of her, secretly pining for Orsino as he pines for Olivia (and as Olivia pines for Viola/Cesario).

The emotional experience Viola describes is one of quiet inaction (as opposed to Orsino's very explicit and very active passion) and so would seem to be influenced by the stereotypical perception in the early modern period of women as the more passive sex. However, Viola also claims that her 'sister' suffered from 'a green and yellow melancholy', which is an eye-catching expression. The explanatory note in the New Cambridge edition of *Twelfth Night* states that a 'green and yellow' pallor was associated with melancholy in the early modern period.[26] The note in the Arden edition of the play, moreover, suggests that this colourful phrase might allude to 'green-sickness', a condition often believed to affect young virgin females, and thus that Viola's (supposed sister's) melancholy may be of a distinctly feminine kind.[27] Yet early modern melancholy was by and large less frequently associated with women than it was with men, not least highborn men such as Orsino. In certain contexts, it was positively fashionable for young noblemen to adopt the sorrowful, pensive expressions and mannerisms associated with melancholy, but it was much less common for women to behave, or to be represented, in similar ways. The question, then, is whether Viola – disguised, as she is for most of the play, as a young man – is challenging Orsino's narrow-minded perception of women's feelings by laying claim to an emotional identity, one that would be familiar to Shakespeare's audiences, from which she, as a woman, would typically be excluded.

The purpose of this section is to explore early modern ideas about melancholy as a contextual and analytical framework for teaching Shakespeare's emotions by using *Twelfth Night* as a case study – and additionally to suggest ways in which students might analyse the relationship between melancholy and gender in the play by asking questions such as the one I have asked above: is Viola's appropriation of emotion conventional or provocatively unconventional in 1602, the year in which *Twelfth Night* was first performed, and what might this tell us about the play?

---

[26] See Donno, 2017, p. 106. In the note, Donno cites a popular treatise on love-related melancholy, Jacques Ferrand's *Erotomania*, written in French in 1610 and translated into English in 1640.

[27] See Elam, 2008, p. 235.

Following an introduction to key aspects of early modern melancholy, the section includes four suggested learning activities, all of which are underpinned by historicism and defamiliarization as productive learning routes for engaging with Shakespearean emotion. The first activity is intended to enhance students' understanding of early modern melancholy by introducing a broader contextual framework, first in the form of a key early modern source on melancholy: Robert Burton's *The Anatomy of Melancholy* first published in 1621. This contextual framework, in turn, may be deployed by teachers and students when working with *Twelfth Night* or with any other of Shakespeare's plays in which melancholy is a notable part of the thematic fabric, including *Romeo and Juliet*, *Love's Labour's Lost*, *The Merchant of Venice*, *As You Like It*, *Hamlet*, *Macbeth* or *Pericles*.

This first activity, moreover, builds on a pedagogical concept introduced to interdisciplinary teaching in the humanities by Shari Tishman. In *Slow Looking: The Art and Practice of Learning Through Observation* (2017), Tishman shows how the exercise of engaging with any kind of object 'slowly' – through sight and other forms of sensory perception – can function as a 'simple' but highly rewarding learning mode. As Tishman writes,

> The definition of slow looking is straightforward. It simply means taking the time carefully to observe more than meets the eye at first glance. [. . .] Whatever sensory form that it takes, slow looking is a way of gaining knowledge about the world. It helps us discern complexities that can't be grasped quickly, and it involves a distinctive set of skills and dispositions that have a different center of gravity than those involved in other modes of learning. (2017, p. 2)

Tishman's framework is also helpful, I will argue, for creating a learning experience in which students engage actively and positively with an unedited and non-modernized early modern text by looking at it 'slowly' – and, importantly, by looking at it as a material object as well as looking at it as a text. Burton's *Anatomy* is unquestionably challenging, not least for students who might be put off by its language, its multiple lengthy Latin citations, its indeterminate genre and structure, and its mammoth length. Yet it also offers an invaluable glimpse into the world of early modern melancholy – *and* it is a beautiful object, not least thanks to the detailed allegorical frontispiece engraved by Christian Le Blon that was added to the 1628 edition. In other words, Burton's *Anatomy* is not only essential to the teaching of early modern melancholy, it is also a fascinating object in its own right, and students, I would argue, will benefit greatly from the opportunity to explore it for themselves. The first activity asks students to look 'slowly' at this book, to take it in and appreciate its unfamiliarity. Practically speaking, this is most easily achieved by bringing a facsimile copy into the classroom, if this is an available option, although I will suggest alternatives when outlining the activity.

The second and third activities build on the first and focus on enhancing students' ability to perform close readings of selected passages from *Twelfth Night*. In the third activity, students are asked to use their acquired knowledge about melancholy from Burton in order to analyse the ways in which key characters in the play – Orsino, Olivia, Viola and Malvolio – each display different kinds of melancholy, while in the final activity students are asked to analyse the ways in which the play's representations of melancholy are related to a gendered discourse. Together, the three learning activities suggest complementary ways in which to teach melancholy as a crucial component in Shakespeare's emotional vocabulary. Melancholy provides an excellent thematic vehicle for teaching several plays comparatively and for crossing the generic boundaries between tragedy, comedy, history, and tragicomedy, since it acquires a role in all of the genres that Shakespeare writes in, including in his poems.[28] The prevalence of melancholy in Shakespeare's creative imagination and in early modern art and culture in general means that it is a topic that has received extensive critical attention: in this section, I offer a necessarily condensed explanation and discussion of the critical field, but I hope in so doing both to offer inspiration to

---

[28] Melancholy and comedy are closely connected in Shakespeare's creative imagination: See Sullivan, 2016, pp. 110–120. See also Bernard (2018) for an extensive discussion on the importance of melancholy to Shakespeare's conception of comedy.

colleagues and to save them time by providing a road map and practical suggestions for where to begin when teaching Shakespearean melancholy. Throughout the section, I refer to and recommend recent scholarly work for further reading and, as in the previous sections, I also include a selection of student-friendly background reading.

Early Modern Melancholy

The early modern understanding of what it was to be 'melancholic', or to suffer from 'melancholy', constitutes one of the most fascinating and, from a modern perspective, productively alienating accounts of emotion in the period. The word 'melancholy' is still in use today, mostly as an adjective: a melancholy person, according to the *Oxford English Dictionary*, may be 'gloomy, mournful, or dejected; inclined to sadness or gloomily or mournfully introspective' (*OED* 3a). However, compared with, say, 'sadness', melancholy is much less commonplace in today's speech and, when used in conversation, might well have a certain old-fashioned ring to it. In the early modern period, however, melancholy, both as an adjective and as a noun, was all the rage. As emotion historians have shown, the interest in melancholy and its effects on those who suffered from it exploded across early modern Europe in a kind of emotional pandemic, with numerous medical and philosophical treatises dedicated to the topic.[29] Robert Burton, in his preface to *The Anatomy of Melancholy*, described the condition as 'a universal malady, an Epidemical disease' ('Democritus Junior to the Reader'), and many other writers, including Shakespeare, were fascinated by melancholy or indeed suffered from melancholy themselves. Painters too helped to establish a visual language of melancholy, while composers such as John Dowland created the period's characteristic melancholic soundscape.

Importantly, melancholy was viewed rather paradoxically both as a physical and mental condition with dangerous, potentially fatal, consequences and also as a marker of intellectual and creative superiority, even genius. Drawing on Platonic and Aristotelian philosophical traditions, the

---

[29] See Trevor, 2004; Gowland, 2006; Lund, 2010, 2021; Bell, 2014; Sullivan, 2016 and 2017; and Bernard, 2018.

fifteenth-century Florentine humanist Marsilio Ficino had claimed a connection between melancholy and intellectual achievement, and this reputation persisted in later explorations of the condition, including in Burton's *Anatomy*. In Ficino's account, melancholy was also associated with the planet Saturn, which lent an astrological explanation to the link between melancholy and genius, since Saturn (both the planet and the classical deity) was associated with contemplation and learning.[30]

When we seek to understand what melancholy meant to Shakespeare and his contemporaries, it is also important to note that early modern melancholy is not exactly an emotion (or a passion), but rather, it is a humour – that is, melancholy was 'black bile', one of the four liquid substances – or humours – that early moderns believed resided in the body, determining an individual's emotional outlook.[31] As Matthew Bell notes, the word 'melancholy' in fact comes from the ancient Greek words 'melainē (black) and cholē (bile)' (2014, p. 39). As I explained in Section 2, when the four humours – blood, phlegm, black bile, and yellow bile – are in healthy balance, so are the body and the mind. However, if the body produces an excess of melancholy or black bile – which might happen during the experience of severe grief – things may start to go very wrong. Among the many and variable symptoms of melancholy in the early modern period, we find both mental delusions and fatal heartbreak. As Erin Sullivan has shown, melancholy-related heartbreak was a frequently registered cause of death in the 'Bills of Mortality' of seventeenth-century London (2013, pp. 933–934). The idea of fatal heartbreak certainly belongs to the era of pre-modern medicine, yet it is not entirely without parallel examples in the twenty-first century. Fascinatingly, some recent scholarship has looked at

---

[30] Ficino sets out his theory in *Three Books of Life* [*De Vita Libri Tres*] (1480–1489), where he draws on the pseudo-Aristotelian *Problems* to suggest a connection between melancholy and geniality. See Ficino in Radden, 2002. For further explanation of Ficino's theory, see Sullivan, 2016, pp. 29–30 and p. 94. On the Aristotelian tradition to Ficino, see also Bernard, 2018, pp. 10–13.

[31] For a helpful explanation of melancholy as a humoral disorder see Sullivan, 2016, pp. 25–30.

early modern representations of heartbreak alongside the twenty-first-century diagnosis of 'Takotsubo syndrome', or TTS, a cardiac condition understood to be caused by acute emotional stress, especially grief.[32] Such historically comparative readings of the ways in which 'grief' has been diagnosed and treated across time is a good example of the potential for interdisciplinary dialogue between emotion history and medicine, which is equally valuable for criticism and in the classroom.

Thus, although early modern melancholy is not in itself an emotion, it is closely linked to emotional experience, especially to the experience of grief, sorrow, sadness, and fear. Love, particularly when unrequited, also has a strong relationship with melancholy, as is evident in the case of Orsino in *Twelfth Night*. Melancholy connects with these emotions because they were understood to potentially cause the overproduction of black bile in the body. Furthermore, because the humoral properties of melancholy were thought to be cold and dry, early moderns worried that excess production might have oppressive effects on the heart, causing it to contract and quite literally dry out. In the *Passions of the Mind in General*, Thomas Wright describes something of this process:

> The cause why sadness doth so move the forces of the body I take to be the gathering together of too much melancholy blood about the heart, which collection extinguisheth the good spirits, or at least dulleth them; besides the heart being possessed of such an humour, cannot digest well the blood and spirits, which ought to be dispersed through the whole body, but converteth them into melancholy, the which humour being cold and dry, drieth the whole body and maketh it wither away; for cold extinguisheth heat, and dryness moisture, which two qualities principally concern life. (1604, E7^{r-v})

---

[32] See Hansen and Philips, 2024. It is beyond the scope of this section to further engage with this topic, but I believe that comparative readings of this kind would have distinct value as a stimulus for discussion in the classroom, not least for teaching purposes in the medical humanities.

Melancholy's ability to extinguish vital heat and dry out moisture in the body is also implied in another early modern text on emotion: Edward Reynolds' *A Treatise of the Passions and Faculties of the Soul of Man* (1640). Writing about grief, Reynolds warns that 'in the body there is no other Passion that doth produce stronger, or more lasting inconveniences by pressure of heart, obstruction of spirit, wasting of strength, dryness of bones, exhausting of Nature' (1640, sig. 2H2^v). From a modern perspective, then, perhaps the simplest way to understand early modern melancholy is as an illness that is closely related to certain emotional states. At the same time, melancholy was clearly much more than an illness in the pathological sense. It was also a multifaceted social identity – a way of being in the world and a way of expressing oneself through emotionally-inflected language and behaviour. In this sense, early modern melancholy should be viewed as a cultural phenomenon – one which not only had a strong presence in literature and drama, painting and music, but which was also shaped and promoted by the arts. When we teach melancholy, we are necessarily teaching at the intersection of medical history and cultural history. In Shakespeare's plays, melancholy is a rich emotional idiom, fashioned from – and responding to – discourses from beyond the world of the theatre, and thus the teaching of Shakespearean melancholy might begin productively by looking at how one of the most widely read texts about melancholy sought to understand the nature of this phenomenon.

Robert Burton's Anatomy of Melancholy

The deep fascination that melancholy held for early modern society is evidenced by the fact that entire books were dedicated to describing and exploring it. Important early modern treatises on melancholy in English include Timothy Bright's *A Treatise of Melancholy* (1586), André du Laurens' *A Discourse of the Preservation of the Sight: of Melancholic Diseases; of Rheums, and of Old Age* (translated from French into English in 1599), and most famously Robert Burton's masterwork *The Anatomy of Melancholy*. This extraordinary book was first published in 1621 in a quarto edition and subsequently in enlarged folio editions in 1624, 1628, 1632, and 1638. Three additional posthumous editions were published in 1651, 1660, and 1676. In other words, *The Anatomy of Melancholy* was already a very popular work in its own time, and it continues to inspire critical and popular enthusiasm today.[33] It is also a very substantial work, literally speaking. As the editors of the modern Oxford edition of *The Anatomy of Melancholy* explain, the first quarto edition of 1621 contained 880 pages and approximately 353,369 words, but Burton continued to add to his work, and by the fourth edition of 1632 the book had grown 'to 822 folio pages and some 505,592 words' (Faulkner, Kiessling, and Blair, 1989, p. xxxix). The sheer size of the *Anatomy* makes it an unwieldy object, and getting to grips with its wide-ranging content is undoubtedly a disorientating experience, which also makes it a challenging text to introduce in the classroom, as I have already noted. Yet at the same time, the *Anatomy* offers great learning potential if students are asked to engage with Burton's book as a manifestation of early modern melancholy in all its wide-ranging 'strangeness'. As I show in the first learning activity of this section, the book itself, as a material object, enables a positive defamiliarizing learning mode – even more so today when so many of our students are used to accessing 'text' only in digital formats.

In the *Anatomy*, Burton describes the many different manifestations and symptoms of melancholy, and he offers copious advice on how to cure the condition; indeed, the *Anatomy* is sometimes described as an early modern 'self-help' book, which may sound reductive but is nonetheless true.[34] Burton makes it clear that he too suffers from the condition, and he is thus an explicitly invested author whose personal voice emerges from the pages, especially in the lengthy preface, where he also explains the reason behind his adopted author persona, 'Democritus Junior', named after the ancient Greek philosopher Democritus of Abdera, who, in an anecdote according to Burton, sought to discover the nature of melancholy. Democritus is pictured in Burton's frontispiece (top centre) surrounded

---

[33] For a comprehensive introduction to *The Anatomy of Melancholy*, see Lund, 2010 and 2021.

[34] For a thoroughgoing and illuminating account of how Burton imagines the curative properties of his book, see Lund, 2010.

by a selection of animals that he has been dissecting for traces of black bile. By writing the *Anatomy*, Burton intends to complete Democritus' task.

What makes the *Anatomy* such a fascinating read is the way in which it combines an intensely learned 'bookishness' and prosaic practicality, for example, when Burton describes the kinds of diet and pastimes either to be avoided or embraced in the attempt to ward off melancholy. To a modern reader, such shifts between tonal register and genre contribute to the overall impression of the *Anatomy* as a thoroughly unfamiliar sort of text. Burton, like many other early modern writers, does not observe the division between disciplines as we do today but moves freely between theology, philosophy, medicine, and literary history. Again, this wide-ranging mode of thinking and writing may feel alienating to twenty-first-century students, but I believe that it can be turned into a positive defamiliarization factor when bringing the *Anatomy* into the classroom. Not only will students have the opportunity to discover a very different understanding of how emotion was experienced in Shakespeare's time, they will hopefully also be able to appreciate the fact that Burton's book, unwieldy as it is, reflects the complexity and importance of emotional experience both then and now.

Burton (1577–1640) lived and worked at Christ Church, one of the colleges of Oxford University, and the *Anatomy* is very much the work of a dedicated scholar; both its content and structure reflect Burton's determination to gather and organize a great deal of material. The book is divided into three main 'Partitions', each of which contains several 'Sections', 'Members', and 'Subsections' – something that also reminds us that this is indeed an 'anatomy' in its meticulous attempt to 'dissect' the condition of melancholy. The first Partition treats primarily the various causes, symptoms, and prognostics of melancholy, and here Burton lists passions such as sorrow, fear, shame, envy, hatred, anger, and several others as causes of melancholy, theorizing each passion at length, which also makes the *Anatomy* a valuable early modern source text on the passions in general. One subsection in the first Partition – to be precise, the fifteenth 'Subsection' of the third 'Member' of the second 'Section' of the first 'Partition' (or, in short, 1.2.3.15) – details the ways in which the '*Love of learning or overmuch study*' may contribute to melancholy, producing symptoms from madness to gout and catarrhs, poor sight and 'winds', which

Burton ascribes to 'overmuch sitting'. Variants of melancholy associated with uncomfortable bowel movements are usually known as hypochondriac melancholy (Burton also calls it 'windy melancholy' and treats it in 1.3.2.2) – 'hypochondria' in this case referring to the area of the abdomen below the ribcage rather than the mental tendency to believe oneself ill. This is a useful reminder for students that early modern medical terminology can mislead the modern reader and that melancholy for early moderns might involve tangibly physical symptoms. Burton follows a common taxonomic distinction between 'head melancholy' – when melancholy is thought to affect the brain – and the kinds of melancholy that were thought to affect the whole body. To a modern reader, 'head melancholy' may be the most familiar-sounding variant, since it fits more readily with our conception of the relationship between emotions and 'mental health', but to Burton and his readers, melancholy could also involve a much cruder bodily experience, including, as he puts it, 'rumbling in the guts' along with 'sowre and sharp belchings' ('Synopsis of the First Partition').[35]

At one point in 1.3.2.2 – 'On windy Hypochondriacal Melancholy' – Burton cites the famed Swiss physician Felix Platter (who, as it happens, was the older half-brother of the Thomas Platter who went to a performance of *Julius Caesar* in London in 1599, as seen in Section 3) on a particularly curious case. In his study of the condition, Platter had come across a man who, having fallen into a water hole in springtime and swallowed some water, was convinced that he had swallowed frogspawn and therefore believed that he had live frogs in his stomach. Platter's diagnosis that he was in fact suffering from 'wind' had no effect. Such is the glorious strangeness of early modern melancholy that it seems to exist along a spectrum from genius to farting, and Burton can be relied on for unexpected examples of all kinds. One way to ensure that students get to experience the richness of early modern melancholy discourse is to set them 'treasure-hunting' for particularly 'strange' and imaginative anecdotes in the *Anatomy*, encouraging them to explore the different subsections in a deliberately unsystematic manner. I would ask them to select a 'favourite'

---

[35] Sullivan provides a helpful analysis of the very physical, including the scatological, aspects of melancholy (2016, chapter 3).

case or example from the book and summarize it in their own words as a short written assignment, either in groups or pairs.

Love Melancholy in Twelfth Night

Burton's second 'Partition' is dedicated to the cure of melancholy with advice on remedies such as the correct diet, exercise, music, and the comforting company of friends. In the third 'Partition', however, Burton turns to the variant of melancholy known as 'love melancholy', which is directly relevant to teaching *Twelfth Night*, since the principal characters in the play – Orsino, Olivia, Viola and Malvolio – all suffer from different versions of this condition. Burton's treatment of love melancholy is very extensive, not least because he devotes a great deal of space to discussing many variants of love itself, but in the second section, he examines so-called 'Heroical Love' – which is perhaps best understood as an overpowering experience of love that may lead to 'lovesickness' or love melancholy. This feeling, like other early modern passions, is situated in the body – specifically, as Burton asserts, 'the part affected in men is the liver' – and, he explains, it is called 'Heroicall, because commonly Gallants & Noble men, the most generous of spirits are possessed with it' (3.2.1.1). This definition clearly applies to Orsino in *Twelfth Night*. 'Heroical love', Burton explains, 'rageth amongst all sorts and conditions of men, but it is most evident amongst such as are young and lusty, in the flower of their years, nobly descended, high fed and such as live idle and at ease' (3.2.1.2). Citing the Islamic philosopher and physician Avicenna, Burton further notes that this kind of love is 'a disease or melancholy vexation or anguish of mind, in which a man continually meditates of the beauty, gesture, manners of his mistress, and troubles himself about it' (3.2.1.2). Again, Orsino is ostensibly at leisure to think of nothing else except Olivia. A certain wryness may be detected in Burton's tone when he further describes the symptoms of the melancholy lover:

> If he get any remnant of hers, a buske-point, a feather of her fan, a shoe-tie, a lace, he weares it for a favour in his hat, or next to his heart. Her picture he adores twice a day, & for two hours together will not look off it; a garter or a bracelet

of hers is more precious than any Saints relic; and he lays it up in his casket, O blessed relic, and every day will kiss it, if in her presence his eye is never off her, & drink where she drank, if it be possible in that very place, &c. If absent, he will sit under that tree where she did use to sit, in that bower, in that very seat, many years after sometimes, and if she be far off, and dwell many miles off, he loves yet to walk that way still, to have his chamber window look that way, to confer with some of her acquaintance, to talk of her, admiring and commending her still and lamenting, honing, wishing himself anything for her sake, to have opportunity to see her, that he might but enjoy her presence [...] Another, he sighs and sobs, & wisheth him a saddle for her to sit on, a posy for her to smell to, & it would not grieve him to be hanged, if he might be strangled in her garters: he would willingly die tomorrow, so that she might kill him with her own hands. (3.2.3.1)

If we compare Burton's description of such behavioural patterns of the melancholy lover with Shakespeare's characterization of Orsino, it becomes easier to see how Orsino treads a fine line between the ennobling feeling, which is one side of 'heroical love', and the kind of obsessive behaviour which comes close to looking ridiculous.

Olivia too shows symptoms associated with the irrational aspects of melancholy caused by 'heroical love' in her relentless pursuit of Viola/ Cesario. She confirms one of the primary causes of love melancholy as described by Burton: namely, that sufferers are often 'infected' through sight: 'the most familiar and usual cause of Love, is that it comes by sight, which conveys those admirable rays of beauty and pleasing graces to the heart' (3.2.2.2). Musing at the speed with which she seems to have caught 'the plague' – that is, love – Olivia confesses 'Methinks I feel this youth's perfections / With an invisible and subtle stealth / To creep in at mine eyes' (1.5.251–53). Viola's love melancholy, however, seems to differ from both Orsino's and Olivia's symptoms. She clearly understands – and knows how to perform – the 'script' of love melancholy: her 'willow cabin' speech to

Olivia in act one, scene five lists typical behaviours of the melancholy lover, some of which echo the behavioural patterns described by Burton. But her own behaviour in respect of Orsino, while characterized by the suffering caused by 'heroical love' – also demonstrates a patience which the other two characters lack, and which is captured in the description of her imagined 'sister' sitting like 'Patience on a monument / Smiling at grief' (2.4.110–11). Thus, while Orsino and Olivia's symptoms largely follow similar patterns, Viola rather resists an easy diagnosis, which works as a reminder that Shakespeare's plays and characters do not always express or represent early modern emotion discourses in a consistent or orthodox manner, as also noted in Section 1. For students, comparing the different behaviours and symptoms of these melancholic characters, and referring to Burton in order to contextualize their observations, is a rewarding learning experience – one which, I believe, significantly enhances their understanding of the play and the ways in which Shakespeare uses melancholy as a dramatic idiom to create characterization and plot.

Malvolio too belongs to the list of melancholic characters in *Twelfth Night*, and in him Shakespeare reproduces some of the symptoms of love melancholy for comic effect. Malvolio is a natural melancholic from the outset of the play – Olivia describes him as 'sad and civil' (3.4.5), but when he is tricked into believing that his mistress loves him, he adopts some of the behaviour of the devoted 'heroical lover'. This clash – between Malvolio's customary sad and grave behaviour and his farcical performance of 'love melancholy' – is usually hilarious in performance. However, the subsequent treatment of Malvolio as 'mad' – with its less than wholly comfortable effect on a modern audience – also draws on the discourse of melancholy. Burton frequently points out that melancholy – including love melancholy – can lead to madness, and when looking at the frontispiece to the *Anatomy*, students will soon notice that the figure of the *inamorato* – the melancholy lover – and the *maniacus* – the melancholy 'madman' are both depicted within the allegorical framework as two sides of the same coin, so to speak. In the comical sub-plot of *Twelfth Night*, Maria and her accomplices can be said to capitalize on the wider cultural and medical association between melancholy and madness in order to play their trick – and get their revenge – on Malvolio. The diagnosis and treatment of Malvolio, then, offers a further angle for exploring the play's negotiation of melancholy in the classroom.

Looking 'Slowly' at Burton's Anatomy of Melancholy: *A Learning Activity*

As I have noted in this section, Burton's *Anatomy* is a fascinating but also a challenging text to introduce in a teaching context. However, this activity suggests a method which is designed to utilize the unfamiliar features of this text – its 'strangeness' – as a productive learning tool. Students are asked to engage with the *Anatomy* as a 'textual object' to be appreciated through a method of 'slow looking' inspired by Shari Tishman's pedagogy, before, in the following activity, they are asked to use Burton's book as a source of information about early modern love melancholy. This first activity also offers a welcome opportunity for students to reflect on the materiality of books and in particular of the books of Shakespeare's day. As well as Tishman's concept of 'slow looking', the approach draws on ideas from the pedagogy known as object-based learning, which is closely related to Tishman's practice and has long been deployed by teachers at several levels, from primary to higher education, especially in subjects related to art history and museum-based teaching. As Helen J. Chatterjee and Leonie Hannan explain in their useful edited collection on object-based learning, the 'object' used by this pedagogical practice refers to a variety of artefacts, and, they note, 'the term could equally apply to manuscripts, rare books and archives' (2015, p. 1). In fact, Chatterjee and Hannan stress the benefits of providing literature students with access to 'textual objects' usually found in libraries and archival collections, arguing that the direct engagement with the materiality of books and texts may 'offer active and experiential learning' (2015, p. 8). Object-based learning is, first and foremost, student-centred and takes as its starting point the students' own experience of the object, as they build meaning by gathering together their observations. It can be highly productive as a collective learning process, demonstrating to students the value of adding and responding to each other's observations. It is often multisensory, involving especially touch (if touching the object is possible and permissible), but it is rooted in sight. As Tishman explains:

> You'll find that once students start generating observations and ideas about an object, it's hard to get them to stop. This is because looking carefully at something and trying to discern its features is a form of cognition with an intrinsically rewarding feedback loop. The more you look, the more you see; the more you see, the more interesting the object becomes. (2008, p. 46)

Importantly, she also points out that object-based learning is often available to students from diverse social backgrounds: 'examining objects directly – either visually, tactually, or aurally – is something most students can do. Regardless of background knowledge, learning style, or skill, almost all students can notice features of an object, ask questions about it, and generate ideas and connections' (2008, p. 46). Few, if any, teachers and students will have access to an actual seventeenth-century edition of Burton's *Anatomy*, but they may have access to a facsimile edition through their institutional library, which will help to give students a sense of the material qualities of Burton's book: its sheer extent, its size and weight, as well as the visual experience of the frontispiece with its allegorical representations of melancholic figures and scenes. If a facsimile edition is not available, I would suggest providing students with a print-out of the frontispiece, which is easily available online on Wikipedia (search for 'Robert Burton, The Anatomy of Melancholy') and tailor the activity to concentrate students' attention solely on this 'object', which is certainly detailed enough to provide the basis for a substantive session of observation and discussion.

Instructions

As preparation for this activity, students should be provided with some contextual knowledge about Burton's book and about early modern melancholy in general, in the form, say, of an introductory lecture or seminar, so they have a number of 'hooks' on which to hang their observations and questions. Whether they are using a facsimile or a print-out of the frontispiece of Burton's book, students should be asked to make as many observations as they can about the 'object'. This is the first and only 'rule' of the activity, and students should be encouraged to work together to listen and to respond to each other's observations, remembering that all observations are 'valid' ones. They should also be encouraged to ask questions about the object – to cultivate a sense of curiosity about it and to wonder at its different features without feeling the necessity to find answers straightaway. The idea, again, is to stay with the primary experience of the object. The setup of the activity depends on the number of students. If working with a relatively small number or a maximum of twenty students, teachers may wish to work with the whole group, facilitating students' experience and observations directly. If working with a larger group, it will usually be more productive to split it into smaller groups of five to six students and circulate between them, prompting them to build on each other's observations (in this case, it will be useful to use both print-outs of the frontispiece for each group and to circulate a facsimile edition between them, if available). After a substantial amount of time dedicated to observing – remembering that the activity is about looking 'slowly' – students should be asked to gather their observations and questions into a short summary of what the 'object' – that is, Burton's book and/or its frontispiece – tells us about melancholy. The aim here is that students will be able to understand and articulate the fact that early modern melancholy can take a great many different forms – for example, from love to madness to scholarly pensiveness – and that Burton's work embodies this complexity both intellectually and in a material sense. Moreover, the aim is for students to reflect on the differences and similarities between early modern melancholy and what they may understand as 'sadness' or 'depression' through an active encounter with a textual object that may at first appear 'strange' and unfamiliar. Finally, the more time students spend actively observing and engaging with Burton's text in a largely self-directed manner, the more natural it will feel for them to begin to read it for information – using it as a source text in the more traditional sense – which is what they are asked to do in the next activity.

Love Melancholy and Gender in Twelfth Night: *Two Learning Activities*

(1) **Comparing the symptoms of love melancholy in Orsino, Olivia, Viola, and Malvolio.** As I have discussed in this section, Shakespeare draws on symptoms and behaviours associated with the kind of 'love melancholy' that Burton describes in the *Anatomy* in the different characterizations of Orsino, Olivia, Viola and Malvolio in *Twelfth Night*. The key aims of this activity are (1) that students should be able to identify the patterns of love melancholy displayed and expressed by each of these characters and discuss the differences between them with nuance and historical insight, and (2) to enhance students' overall understanding of the play through its dramatization of melancholy. Finally, on a more general level, this activity trains students in the key historicist skill of working with a contemporaneous non-literary source in order to contextualize their reading of a literary one, in this case a Shakespearean play, while also recognising that the difference between 'literary' and 'non-literary' in texts from Shakespeare's time may not be as clear as they might assume.

Instructions

Students should be asked to close-read Burton on the symptoms of love melancholy in 3.2.3.1 of *The Anatomy of Melancholy* – that is, the third partition, section 2, member 3, subsection 1 – and list as many of the symptoms Burton describes, both physical and behavioural, as they can. Given the length of this passage, I would suggest dividing it into smaller portions and asking students to work in groups with one portion only. The findings of each group may then be gathered to make a shared list or shared directly by using a digital tool such as 'Padlet'. The shared list may be discussed in class to support students' understanding of Burton's language and descriptions, which will make the next part of the activity more straightforward and rewarding. Using the list, students may try to 'diagnose' each of the four characters – Orsino, Olivia, Viola and Malvolio – comparing Shakespeare's representation of melancholy with Burton's and noting differences between characters. This may also be done in groups and, if there is not sufficient time for the groups to work on each character, they may focus on one character each and present their reading to the rest of the class as part of a summarizing discussion. The format of the activity is thus flexible and adaptable, but the basic premise – close-reading the play for its different representations of melancholy and using Burton to contextualize and historicize these representations – remains key. This activity works well as a preparation for the next activity, which extends the close reading to include a focus on gender and melancholy and the ways in which Shakespeare explores this relationship in the play.

(2) **Melancholy and Gender in *Twelfth Night*.** In *Twelfth Night*, Orsino seems to insist that his love melancholy is ennobled by his gender – that the strength of his feelings has to do with the fact that they are inherently masculine. In the speech that I cited at the opening of this section, Orsino claims that,

> There is no woman's sides
> Can bide the beating of so strong a passion
> As love doth give my heart; no woman's heart
> So big, to hold so much. They lack retention.
> Alas, their love may be called appetite,
> No motion of the liver, but the palate,
> That suffers surfeit, cloyment, and revolt,
> But mine is as hungry as the sea,
> And can digest as much. Make no compare
> Between that love a woman can bear me,
> And that I owe Olivia.
>
> (2.4.89–99)

As Cora Fox explains, Orsino's understanding of his own masculine emotion as far greater and nobler than what a woman might feel draws on early modern ideas of the humoral body. A woman's weaker body and smaller heart cannot produce or contain as strong a passion as can Orsino's larger and stronger heart.[36] *His* love is a 'motion of the liver', an internal organ which, like the heart, played a crucial role as a location of the passions in the

---

[36] See Fox, 2022, p. 215.

humoral body, whereas women's more superficial love is only associated with the 'palate', that is with the mouth or taste.[37] Moreover, Orsino's view of women as lacking 'retention' is a direct reference to the female humoral body as an overly moist and 'leaky vessel' that is unable to contain and control its fluids, such as menstrual blood and tears.[38] The key point here, as Fox also observes, is that Orsino's language – dependent as it is on contemporaneous ideas about the human body – reveals an understanding of emotion that is distinctly gendered (2022, p. 215). Within this discursive framework, women's emotions are secondary to men's emotions. However, when reading the play together with students, an important question to ask is whether (and how) Shakespeare's text endorses or resists this gendered perception of emotion. Shakespeare's representation of Orsino's love (and his love melancholy) is certainly ambivalent with plenty of potential for making the count look ridiculous, especially when we read the play alongside Burton's description of the obsessive behaviour of such lovers, as we have already seen in this section. The aim of this final learning activity, then, is for students to investigate the ways in which *Twelfth Night* negotiates the relationship between emotion – specifically love and love melancholy – and gender, focusing on a close-reading of Orsino's speech (2.4.89–99) and encouraging students to relate it to any other moments in the play where emotion appears to be defined by gender and vice versa.

Instructions

Students will need some contextual knowledge about the humoral body for this activity, either in the form of an introductory lecture or background reading (Fox's essay is very helpful). Working in pairs or small groups, they should then be asked to close read Orsino's speech (2.4.89–99) and make notes on how he distinguishes between masculine and feminine emotion, relating their reading to the ways in which he describes bodily differences between men and women. Students should note the humoral

---

[37] Ibid.

[38] Gail Kern Paster has shown the pervasiveness of the 'leaky vessel' trope in early modern (patriarchal) thinking: see Paster, 1998, esp. chapter one.

vocabulary of the speech and suggest explanations for Orsino's claims that women's hearts are smaller, that 'they lack retention', that their palate soon 'suffers surfeit', whereas the digestive capacities of his love are unlimited. When students have a good grasp of Orsino's humoral vocabulary, they should then be asked to read his speech 'against the grain', asking whether the audience will take Orsino's claims at face value or whether there is room for a more resistant interpretation. Students may note the potential irony in Orsino's instruction to Viola 'to make no comparison' between his masculine love and the love that women may feel, since such a comparison is in fact the basis for his own arguments. They may also wish to refer to Viola's defence of women's love in her ostensibly masculine response: 'We men may say more, swear more, but indeed / Our shows are more than will: for still we prove / Much in our vows, but little in our love' (2.4.112–14). Questions to prompt students' reading might include:

(1) How does Viola's representation of women's love (in which she also refers to her imaginary melancholy sister) contradict Orsino's humoral understanding of gendered emotion?
(2) Does she rely on the same humoral vocabulary as he uses, or does she introduce a different discursive framework into the debate about gender and emotion?
(3) How is her (sister's) love melancholy different from his?

This activity is thus intended to enhance students' understanding of the play and of Shakespeare's negotiation of emotion and gender by way of a two-step close-reading analysis: one which asks students first to relate the emotional vocabulary of the play to the specific historical context of the humours and to early modern understandings of male and female bodies, and which then asks students to investigate how Shakespeare potentially subverts these ideas and their inbuilt gendered prejudice.

Background Reading

Bernard, J.F. (2017). *Shakespearean Melancholy: Philosophy, Form and the Transformation of Comedy* (esp. introduction and Chapter 4), Edinburgh: Edinburgh University Press.

Fox, Cora. (2022). 'Gender, Emotion, Literature: "No Woman's Heart" in Shakespeare's *Twelfth Night*'. In Patrick Colm Hogan, Bradley J. Irish, and Lalita Pandit Hogan, eds., *The Routledge Companion to Literature and Emotion*, London: Routledge, pp. 214–224.

Gowland, Angus. (2006). 'The Problem of Early Modern Melancholy'. *Past and Present* 191, 77–120.

Lund, Mary Ann. (2010). *Melancholy, Medicine and Religion in Early Modern England: Reading The Anatomy of Melancholy* (esp. 'Introduction'), Cambridge: Cambridge University Press.

Lund, Mary Ann. (2021). *A User's Guide to Melancholy* (esp. 'Introduction' and Part 2, Section 5 'Love and Sex'), Cambridge: Cambridge University Press.

Sullivan, Erin. (2016). *Beyond Melancholy: Sadness in Renaissance England* (esp. 'Introduction' and Chapter 3), Oxford: Oxford University Press

Sullivan, Erin. (2017). 'Melancholy'. In Susan Broomhall, ed., *Early Modern Emotions: An Introduction*, London: Routledge, pp. 56–61.

Conclusion

When we teach Shakespeare's plays, it is easy to take their emotional content for granted. Emotions, as I began this Element by stating, are everywhere in the plays, and therefore they may in fact become invisible to us. This, I believe, is especially true if we do not read Shakespeare's dramatization of emotions through the same historically-inspired lens that we apply to many other aspects of his writing. We may feel that we already know or understand Shakespeare's emotions, not least if we have been taught to believe that they are directly accessible to us. Because the emotions of Shakespeare's characters are relatively easy to identify – when one of his characters is angry, for instance, we, as readers and audiences, are usually able to detect that anger in the dialogue – Shakespeare's emotional world may not feel very remote at all. Shakespeare's characters are good at expressing their emotions; they tell us when they are angry, and they also often tell us why, so it is in many ways natural for us to feel that we 'understand' their emotions. However, as I have tried to show in this Element, we may not always understand *how* they feel their emotions, unless we are able to situate those emotions within Shakespeare's own historical and cultural moment.

Letting go of the idea of direct emotional communion with Shakespeare – the idea that Shakespeare was somehow able to intuit a universal and transhistorical framework for human feelings – might be challenging, both for teachers and for students. There might be an unspoken fear in the classroom that Shakespeare ceases to be 'relevant' to students if he is no longer held up as a writer with the most astonishing ability to express their emotions. Yet there is, as I hope I have shown, so much more to be gained from understanding Shakespearean emotions in all their wonderful, unfamiliar complexity and diversity. Perhaps Shakespeare's chief relevance is in fact enabled when his plays help us understand, not that we all know what it is like to love, or hate, or feel sad, but that we all feel such feelings *differently* – and would have felt them even more differently if we had been born a hundred, or four hundred, years earlier. And in turn, recognizing such emotional difference might help us to turn the Shakespearean classroom into an increasingly tolerant and inclusive affective space. It is my hope that the teaching tools offered by this Element will contribute to making this possible.

References

Primary Reading

Bright, Timothy. (1586). *A Treatise on Melancholy*, London.

Burton, Robert. (1621). *The Anatomy of Melancholy*, London.

Coeffeteau, Nicholas. (1621). *A Table of Human Passions*, translated from French into English by Edward Grimeston, London.

Laurens, André du. (1599). *A Discourse of the Preservation of the Sight: Of Melancholic Diseases; of Rheums, and of Old Age*, London.

Reynolds, Edward. (1640). *A Treatise of the Passions and Faculties of the Soul of Man*, London.

Rogers, Thomas. (1576). *A Philosophical Discourse Entitled the Anatomy of the Mind*, London.

Shakespeare, William. (1597). *Romeo and Juliet*, 3rd ed., edited by G. Blakemore Evans (2023), Cambridge: Cambridge University Press.

Shakespeare, William. (c.1599). *Julius Caesar*, 3rd ed., edited by Martin Spevack (2017), Cambridge: Cambridge University Press.

Shakespeare, William. (c.1600). *Twelfth Night*, 3rd ed., edited by Elizabeth Donno (2024), Cambridge: Cambridge University Press.

Wright, Thomas. (1604) *The Passions of the Mind in General*, London.

Secondary Reading

Barclay, Katie. (2017). 'Space and Place'. In Susan Broomhall, ed., *Early Modern Emotions: An Introduction*, London: Routledge, pp. 20–23.

Barclay, Katie. (2020). *The History of Emotions: A Student Guide to Methods and Sources*, London: Bloomsbury.

Barclay, Katie. (2021). 'State of the Field: The History of Emotions'. *History* 106(71), 456–466.

References

Bell, Matthew. (2014). *Melancholia: The Western Malady*, Cambridge: Cambridge University Press.

Bernard, J. F. (2018). *Shakespearean Melancholy: Philosophy, Form and the Transformation of Comedy*, Edinburgh: Edinburgh University Press.

Boddice, Rob. (2023). *The History of Emotions*, 2nd ed., Manchester: Manchester University Press.

Broomhall, Susan, ed. (2017). *Early Modern Emotions: An Introduction*, New York: Routledge.

Chatterjee, Helen J., and Hannan, Leonie, eds. (2015). *Engaging the Senses: Object-Based Learning in Higher Education*, London: Routledge.

Clough, Patricia Ticineto, and Halley, Jean, eds. (2007). *The Affective Turn: Theorizing the Social*, Durham: Duke University Press.

Craik, Katharine A. ed., (2020). *Shakespeare and Emotion*, Cambridge: Cambridge University Press.

Cummings, Brian, and Sierhuis, Freya, eds. (2013). *Passions and Subjectivity in Early Modern Culture*, Farnham: Ashgate.

Dadabhoy, Ambereen, and Mehdizadeh, Nedda. (2023). *Anti-Racist Shakespeare*, Cambridge Elements: Shakespeare and Pedagogy, Cambridge: Cambridge University Press.

Dawson, Lesel. (2008). *Lovesickness and Gender in Early Modern English Literature*, Oxford: Oxford University Press.

Dixon, Thomas. (2003). *From Passions to Emotions: The Creation of a Secular Psychological Category*, Cambridge: Cambridge University Press.

Dixon, Thomas. (2020). 'What Is the History of Anger a History of?' *Emotions: History, Culture, Society* 4(1), 1–34.

Dixon, Thomas. (2023). *The History of Emotions: A Very Short Introduction*, Oxford: Oxford University Press.

Eklund, Hillary, and Hyman, Wendy Beth, eds. (2019). *Teaching Social Justice through Shakespeare: Why Renaissance Literature Matters Now*, Edinburgh: Edinburgh University Press.

Enterline, Lynn. (2012). *Shakespeare's Schoolroom: Rhetoric, Discipline, Emotion*, Philadelphia: University of Pennsylvania Press.

Escolme, Bridget. (2014). *Emotional Excess on the Shakespearean Stage*, London: Arden Shakespeare.

Faulkner, Thomas C., Kiessling, Nicolas K., and Blair, Rhonda L., eds. (1989). *Robert Burton, The Anatomy of Melancholy*, Vols. I–VI, Oxford: Oxford University Press.

Fox, Cora. (2022). 'Gender, Emotion, Literature: "No Woman's Heart" in Shakespeare's *Twelfth Night*'. In Patrick Colm Hogan, Bradley J. Irish, and Lalita Pandit Hogan, eds., *The Routledge Companion to Literature and Emotion*, London: Routledge, pp. 214–224.

Fox, Cora, Irish, Bradley J., and Miura, Cassie M., eds. (2021). *Positive Emotions in Early Modern Literature and Culture*, Manchester: Manchester University Press.

Gibson, Rex. (2016). *Teaching Shakespeare: A Handbook for Teachers*, Cambridge School Shakespeare, 2nd ed., Cambridge: Cambridge University Press.

Gowland, Angus. (2006). 'The Problem of Early Modern Melancholy'. *Past and Present* 191(1), 77–120.

Gowland, Angus. (2024). 'Hamlet's Melancholy Imagination', *Shakespeare*, 1–20. https://doi.org/10.1080/17450918.2024.2334858 (accessed 18 December 2024).

Hansen, Claire, and Philips, Bríd. (2024). '"Whilt Break My Heart?" Takotsubo Syndrome and Shakespeare's Discourse of Heartbreak in *Antony and Cleopatra* and *King Lear*, *Shakespeare*, 1–24. https://doi.org/10.1080/17450918.2024.2319124 (accessed 18 December 2024).

Hobgood, Allison P. (2014). *Passionate Playgoing in Early Modern England*, Cambridge: Cambridge University Press.

Irish, Bradley J. (2023). *Shakespeare and Disgust: The History and Science of Early Modern Revulsion*, London: Arden Shakespeare.

Jeffrey, David. (2021). 'Shakespeare's Empathy: Enhancing Connection in the Patient-Doctor Relationship in Times of Crisis', *Journal of the Royal Society of Medicine* 114(4), 178–181.

Kambaskovic, Danijela. (2017). 'Humoral Theory'. In Susan Broomhall, ed., *Early Modern Emotions: An Introduction*, London: Routledge, pp. 39–42.

LaPerle, Carol Mejia. (2019). '"If I Might Have My Will": Aaron's Affect and Race in *Titus Andronicus*'. In Farah Karim-Cooper, ed., *Titus Andronicus: The State of Play*, London: Arden Shakespeare, pp. 135–156.

LaPerle, Carol Mejia, ed. (2022). *Race and Affect in Early Modern English Literature*, Tempe: Arizona Center for Medieval and Renaissance Studies Press.

Lemmings, David, and Brooks, Ann. (2014). 'The Emotional Turn in the Humanities and Social Sciences'. In David Lemmings and Ann Brooks, eds., *Emotions and Social Change: Historical and Sociological Perspectives*, London: Routledge, pp. 3–18.

Leys, Ruth. (2017). *The Ascent of Affect: Genealogy and Critique*, Chicago: University of Chicago Press.

Low, Jennifer A., and Myhill, Nova, eds. (2011). *Imagining the Audience in Early Modern Drama, 1558–1642*, New York: Palgrave Macmillan.

Lund, Mary Ann. (2010). *Melancholy, Medicine and Religion in Early Modern England: Reading the Anatomy of Melancholy*, Cambridge: Cambridge University Press.

Lund, Mary Ann. (2021). *A User's Guide to Melancholy*, Cambridge: Cambridge University Press.

McCarthy, Harry, in collaboration with Judy Bae. (2025). *Shakespeare's Stages*, Cambridge: Cambridge University Press.

Meek, Richard, and Sullivan, Erin, eds. (2015). *The Renaissance of Emotion: Understanding Affect in Shakespeare and His Contemporaries*, Manchester: Manchester University Press.

Menzer, Paul. (2011). 'Crowd Control'. In Jennifer A. Low and Nova Myhill, eds., *Imagining the Audience in Early Modern Drama, 1558–1642*, New York: Palgrave Macmillan, pp. 19-36.

Pang, Nicholas Tze Ping, Thrichelvam, Nathisha, and Wider, Walton. (2023). 'Shakespeare as a vehicle for empathy and diagnostic skills training in undergraduate medical students in their psychiatry posting'. *Frontiers in Education* 8:1045069, 1–6.

Panjwani, Varsha. (2022). *Podcasts and Feminist Shakespeare Pedagogy*, Cambridge Elements: Shakespeare and Pedagogy, Cambridge: Cambridge University Press.

Paster, Gail Kern. (1993). *The Body Embarrassed: Drama and the Disciplines of Shame in Early Modern England*, Ithaca New York: Cornell University Press.

Paster, Gail Kern. (1998). 'Unbearable Coldness of Female Being: Women's Imperfection and the Humoral Economy'. *English Literary Renaissance* 29(3), 416–440.

Paster, Gail Kern. (2004). *Humoring the Body: Emotions and the Shakespearean Stage*, Chicago: Chicago University Press.

Paster, Gail Kern. (2020). 'Communities: *Julius Caesar*'. In Katharine Craik, ed., *Shakespeare and Emotion*, Cambridge: Cambridge University Press, pp. 94–108.

Paster, Gail Kern, Rowe, Katherine, and Floyd-Wilson, Mary, eds. (2004). *Reading the Early Modern Passions: Essays in the Cultural History of Emotion*, Philadelphia: University of Pennsylvania Press.

Pollard, Tanya. (2020). 'Audiences: *Much Ado about Nothing*, *Measure for Measure*'. In Katharine Craik, ed., *Shakespeare and Emotion*, Cambridge: Cambridge University Press, pp. 109–121.

Rhodes, Neil. (2020). 'Rhetoric: *Titus Andronicus*, *Julius Caesar*'. In Katharine Craik, ed., *Shakespeare and Emotion*, Cambridge: Cambridge University Press, pp. 19–33.

Robinson, Benedict S. (2020). 'Feeling Feelings in Early Modern England'. In Alex Houen, ed., *Affect and Literature*, Cambridge: Cambridge University Press, pp. 213–228.

Robinson, Benedict S. (2021). *Passion's Fictions from Shakespeare to Richardson: Literature and the Sciences of Soul and Mind*, Oxford: Oxford University Press.

Rosenwein, Barbara H. (2006). *Emotional Communities in the Early Middle Ages*, Ithaca: Cornell University Press.

Rowe, Katherine. (2003). 'Minds in Company: Shakespearean Tragic Emotions'. In Richard Dutton and Jean E. Howard, eds., *A Companion to Shakespeare's Works, Vol. I, The Tragedies*, Oxford: Blackwell, pp. 47–72.

Schoenfeldt, Michael C. (1999). *Bodies and Selves in Early Modern England: Physiology and Inwardness in Spenser, Shakespeare, Herbert, and Milton*, Cambridge: Cambridge University Press.

Shakespeare, William. (c.1599). *Julius Caesar*, edited by David Daniell (1998), London: Arden Shakespeare.

Shakespeare, William. (c.1600). *Twelfth Night*, edited by Keir Elam (2008), London: Arden Shakespeare.

Smith, Bruce. (2004). 'E/loco/com/motion'. In Peter Holland and Stephen Orgel, eds., *From Script to Stage in Early Modern England*, New York: Palgrave, pp. 131–150.

Steenbergh, Kristine. (2022). 'How (Not) to love and Anemone: Animal, Vegetal, and Mineral Intimacies in Shakespeare's *Venus and Adonis*'. *Esprit Createur*, 62(4), 25–39.

Steggle, Matthew. (2007). *Laughing and Weeping in Early Modern Theatres*, London: Routledge.

Steggle, Matthew. (2018). 'The Humours in Humour: Shakespeare and Early Modern Psychology'. In Heather Hirschfeld, ed., *The Oxford*

Handbook of Shakespearean Comedy, Oxford: Oxford University Press, pp. 220–235.

Stern, Tiffany. (2004). *Making Shakespeare: From Stage to Page*, London: Routledge.

Stow, John. (1633). *A Survey of London*, London.

Sullivan, Erin. (2013). 'Shakespeare and the History of Heartbreak'. *The Lancet* 382(9896), 933–934.

Sullivan, Erin. (2016). *Beyond Melancholy: Sadness in Renaissance England*, Oxford: Oxford University Press.

Sullivan, Erin. (2017). 'Melancholy'. In Susan Broomhall, ed., *Early Modern Emotions: An Introduction*, London: Routledge, pp. 56–61.

Thompson, Ayanna, and Turchi, Laura. (2016). *Teaching Shakespeare with Purpose: A Student-Centred Approach*, London: Bloomsbury.

Tishman, Shari. (2008). 'The Object of Their Attention'. *Educational Leadership* 65(5), 44–46.

Tishman, Shari. (2017). *Slow Looking: The Art and Practice of Learning Through Observation*, New York: Routledge.

Trevor, Douglas. (2004). *The Poetics of Melancholy in Early Modern England*, Cambridge: Cambridge University Press.

Wells, Marion A. (2023). *Gender, Affect, and Emotion from Classical to Early Modern Literature: Afterlives of the Nightingale's Song*, Cham, Switzerland: Palgrave Macmillan.

Whipday, Emma. (2023). *Teaching Shakespeare and His Sisters: An Embodied Approach*, Cambridge Elements: Shakespeare and Pedagogy, Cambridge: Cambridge University Press.

White, R. S., Houlahan, Mark, and O'Loughlin, Katrina, eds. (2015). *Shakespeare and Emotions: Inheritances, Enactments, Legacies*, New York: Palgrave Macmillan.

Websites

'Early English Books Online Collections' by the University of Michigan Library. https://quod.lib.umich.edu/e/eebogroup/.

'EarlyPrint: Curating and Exploring Early Printed English' by Northwestern University and Washington University in St. Louis. https://earlyprint.org/.

'Emotions Lab' by the Centre for the History of the Emotions at Queen Mary University of London. (2019). https://emotionslab.org/.

'The Forest of Rhetoric (silva rhetoricae)' by Gideon Burton (Brigham Young University) https://rhetoric.byu.edu.

French, Esther. (2016). Balancing the body and consulting the heavens: Medicine in.

Shakespeare's time'. The Folger Shakespeare Library. www.folger.edu/blogs/shakespeare-and-beyond/elizabethan-medicine-shakespeare/.

'History of Emotions – Insights into Research' by the Center for the History of Emotions at the Max Planck Institute. (2013). www.history-of-emotions.mpg.de/en.

Lyon, Karen. (2015). 'The Four Humors: Eating in the Renaissance'. The Folger Shakespeare.

Library. www.folger.edu/blogs/shakespeare-and-beyond/the-four-humors-eating-in-the-renaissance/.

'Map of Early Modern London (MoEML)' by the University of Victoria. https://mapoflondon.uvic.ca/.

'Melancholy: A New Anatomy' at the Bodleian Library, University of Oxford (Exhibition 29 September 2021 – 20 March 2022). https://visit.bodleian.ox.ac.uk/event/melancholy-new-anatomy.

Padlet. https://padlet.com/.

'Panorama of London by Claes Van Visscher (1616)' on Wikimedia Commons. https://commons.wikimedia.org/wiki/File:Panorama_of_London_by_Claes_Van_Visscher,_1616.jpg.

'Robert Burton's Anatomy of Melancholy, frontispiece to the 1628 edition' on Wikipedia. https://en.wikipedia.org/wiki/The_Anatomy_of_Melancholy#/media/File:Robert_Burton's_Anatomy_of_Melancholy,_1626,_2nd_edition.jpg.

'The Swan after a drawing by Johannes de Witt' on Wikimedia Commons. https://commons.wikimedia.org/wiki/File:The_Swan_cropped.png.

'Sources of Early Modern Emotion in English 1500–1700 (SEMEE)'. www.earlymodernemotion.net/.

US National Library of Medicine. (2012–2022-present). '"And there's the humor of it!": Shakespeare and the Four Humors' (online exhibition). www.nlm.nih.gov/exhibition/shakespeare-and-the-four-humors/index.html.

Quintillian. (2006). *Institutes of Oratory*. Ed.Lee Honeycutt. Trans. John Selby Watson. Iowa State. http://kairos.technorhetoric.net/stasis/2017/honeycutt/quintilian/.

Acknowledgements

I am deeply grateful to the 'Shakespeare and Pedagogy' series general editors Gillian Woods and Liam Semler for supporting this volume and to Gillian for her generous and thorough help with the writing and revising process. I also owe great thanks to the peer reviewer for their highly helpful comments. Not least, I am eternally grateful to all the students whom I have had the great luck and privilege to teach.

For my parents: my first teachers

Cambridge Elements

Shakespeare and Pedagogy

Liam E. Semler

The University of Sydney

Liam E. Semler is Professor of Early Modern Literature in the Department of English at the University of Sydney. He is author of Teaching Shakespeare and Marlowe: Learning versus the System (2013) and co-editor (with Kate Flaherty and Penny Gay) of Teaching Shakespeare beyond the Centre: Australasian Perspectives (2013). He is editor of Coriolanus: A Critical Reader (2021) and co-editor (with Claire Hansen and Jackie Manuel) of Reimagining Shakespeare Education: Teaching and Learning through Collaboration (Cambridge, forthcoming). His most recent book outside Shakespeare studies is The Early Modern Grotesque: English Sources and Documents 1500–1700 (2019). Liam leads the Better Strangers project which hosts the open-access Shakespeare Reloaded website (shakespearereloaded.edu.au).

Gillian Woods

University of Oxford

Gillian Woods is an Associate Professor and Tutorial Fellow in English at Magdalen College, University of Oxford. She is the author of *Shakespeare's Unreformed Fictions* (2013; joint winner of Shakespeare's Globe Book Award), *Romeo and Juliet: A Reader's Guide to Essential Criticism* (2012), and numerous articles about Renaissance drama. She is the co-editor (with Sarah Dustagheer) of *Stage Directions and Shakespearean Theatre* (2018). She is currently working on a new edition of

A Midsummer Night's Dream for Cambridge University Press, as well as a Leverhulme-funded monograph about Renaissance Theatricalities. As founding director of the Shakespeare Teachers' Conversations, she runs a seminar series that brings together university academics, school teachers and educationalists from non-traditional sectors, and she regularly runs workshops for schools.

ADVISORY BOARD

Janelle Jenstad, *University of Victoria*

Farah Karim-Cooper, *Shakespeare's Globe*

Bi-qi Beatrice Lei, *National Taiwan University*

Florence March, *Université Paul-Valéry Montpellier*

Peggy O'Brien, *Folger Shakespeare Library*

Paul Prescott, *University of California Merced*

Abigail Rokison-Woodall, *University of Birmingham*

Emma Smith, *University of Oxford*

Patrick Spottiswoode, *Shakespeare's Globe*

Jenny Stevens, *English Association*

Ayanna Thompson, *Arizona State University*

Joe Winston, *University of Warwick*

About the Series

The teaching and learning of Shakespeare around the world is complex and changing. Elements in Shakespeare and Pedagogy synthesises theory and practice, including provocative, original pieces of research, as well as dynamic, practical engagements with learning contexts.

Cambridge Elements

Shakespeare and Pedagogy

ELEMENTS IN THE SERIES

Anti-Racist Shakespeare
Ambereen Dadabhoy and Nedda Mehdizadeh

Teaching Shakespeare and His Sisters: An Embodied Approach
Emma Whipday

Shakespeare and Place-Based Learning
Claire Hansen

Critical Pedagogy and Active Approaches to Teaching Shakespeare
Jennifer Kitchen

Teaching with Interactive Shakespeare Editions
Laura B. Turchi

Disavowing Authority in the Shakespeare Classroom
Huw Griffiths

The Pedagogy of Watching Shakespeare
Bethan Marshall, Myfanwy Edwards and Charlotte Dixie

Teaching English as a Second Language with Shakespeare
Fabio Ciambella

Shakespeare and Neurodiversity
Laura Seymour

Transdisciplinary Shakespeare Pedagogy
Coen Heijes

Teaching Shakespeare's Theatre of the World
Kristen Abbott Bennett

Teaching Shakespeare's Emotions
Anne Sophie Refskou

A full series listing is available at: www.cambridge.org/ESPG

For EU product safety concerns, contact us at Calle de José Abascal, 56–1°, 28003 Madrid, Spain or eugpsr@cambridge.org.

www.ingramcontent.com/pod-product-compliance
Lightning Source LLC
LaVergne TN
LVHW011848060526
838200LV00054B/4228